Twayne's English Authors Series

Sylvia E. Bowman, *Editor*

INDIANA UNIVERSITY

John Henry Newman

(TEAS) 140

John Henry Newman

By AMERICO D. LAPATI
The Catholic University of America

Twayne Publishers, Inc. :: New York

To My Students
who have given me a keen appreciation
of the dual role of spiritual and
intellectual guide so ably lived by
John Henry Newman

Preface

No one can deny that John Henry Newman holds a place of respect in English literature. Hardly an anthology neglects to include some selection from his prose or poetry, and books and studies about him abound. Despite his partisanship as a Roman Catholic writer, much of his thought transcends any particular religious tenet. Even many of his religious views appeal to man's basic aspirations towards God and concern man's relations to his Creator. His thought on nonreligious matters may be said to have a universal appeal; his religious thought, an ecumenical one. Newman wrote only when he felt a "call" to set forth his ideas. Events, false charges, deliberate distortions of truth—all served as a stimulus for writing. The standard edition of Newman's collected works totals forty volumes; but he wrote not for literary fame, financial reward, or merely for the joy of writing. Duty to truth alone was his motive.

The study and reading of Newman's works, however, have been selective for the most part. He is widely known for his *Apologia* and *The Idea of a University* in prose; for "The Pillar of the Cloud" and *The Dream of Gerontius* in poetry; for a few sermons. Students of theology are acquainted with his *Essay on the Development of Christian Doctrine*. Since much more by this forceful personality and thinker of nineteenth-century England remains to be read and studied, and since knowledge of Newman is selective and limited, this study offers an introduction to the "whole" Newman: the writer, the thinker, the man.

Because of the plethora of Newman's own works and works about him, it becomes a herculean task for those unacquainted with him even to find a starting-point for their study. Consequently, this book offers a compact résumé of Newman's life and writings, with a brief appraisal of their significance in his career and their effect on future thought and events. But the "whole"

Newman is presented with no pretension that herein is a definitive and complete survey of Newman. Rather, I hope that this compact introduction will lead the reader to delve more deeply into the fascinating details of Newman's life and, more importantly, to penetrate into his thought by reading his original works.

Grateful acknowledgment is made to the Very Reverend Mariner T. Smith, O.P., J.C.D., S.T.M., late Professor of Theology, Providence College, Providence, Rhode Island, for his reading of the manuscript and for his valuable suggestions and criticisms.

AMERICO D. LAPATI

Washington, D.C.
January, 1971

Contents

Contents

Chronology

1801 John Henry Newman born in London, England, February 21, son of John Newman and Jemima Fourdrinier.

1808 Entered Ealing School.

1817 Entered Trinity College, Oxford.

1819 Collaborated with William Bowden on periodical *The Undergraduate* and on the poem "St. Bartholomew's Eve."

1822 Elected Fellow at Oriel College, Oxford.

1824 Ordained deacon on June 13. Assigned curate, St. Clement's Church, Oxford.

1825 Ordained to Anglican priesthood on May 29. Vice-principal of Alban Hall.

1826 Public tutor at Oriel College.

1827 Public Examiner in Classics, Oxford University.

1828 Vicar of St. Mary's Church, Oxford.

1832 Wrote *The Arians in the Fourth Century;* not published until 1833.

1832– Made tour of the Mediterranean; wrote verses for the
1833 *British Magazine.*

1833 Beginning of Oxford Movement. Publication of *Tracts for the Times* begins and continues to 1841.

1836 *Lyra Apostolica* published. Editor of *British Critic.*

1837 *The Prophetical Office of the Church.*

1838 *Lectures on Justification.*

1841 Publication of famous Tract 90.

1842 Left Oxford for Littlemore.

1843 Resigned from St. Mary's, Oxford.

1844 Wrote *Essay on the Development of Christian Doctrine.*

1845 Converted to Roman Catholicism.

1846 Visited Rome.

1847 Ordained to Roman Catholic priesthood on May 30; returned to England.

1848 *Loss and Gain.*
1849 *Discourses to Mixed Congregations.*
1850 *Lectures on Certain Difficulties Felt by Anglicans.*
1851 *Lectures on the Present Position of Catholics in England.*
1852 The Achilli trial. Lectures *The Idea of a University* delivered in Ireland.
1854 Inaugurated as rector of the Catholic University of Ireland; served until 1858.
1855 *Callista,* begun in 1849, completed and published.
1856 *The Office and Work of Universities* published.
1857 Received official invitation to supervise a new English translation of the Bible.
1858 Adviser to *Atlantis,* a magazine.
1859 Editor of *Rambler* magazine.
1864 The *Apologia* written.
1865 *Dream of Gerontius* published.
1866 *Letter to Pusey,* written in 1865, published.
1868 *Verses on Various Occasions.*
1870 The *Grammar of Assent.*
1872 *Historical Sketches.*
1875 *Letter to the Duke of Norfolk. Tracts for the Times* revised.
1878 Elected Honorary Fellow of Trinity College, Oxford.
1879 Appointed cardinal by Pope Leo XIII.
1890 Died on August 11.

CHAPTER 1

The Making of the Scholar and Leader

I Early Formative Years

JOHN HENRY NEWMAN was born on February 21, 1801, in London, England. His father John was the member of a banking family; his mother Jemima Fourdrinier was the descendent of a French Protestant family that had left France for England when the Edict of Nantes was revoked in 1685. As members of the Church of England, John Henry was baptized in the Anglican Church of St. Benet Fink on April 9, 1801.[1]

The Newmans then lived on Old Broad Street, London, where John Henry spent his childhood days, except for six years when the family lived at Grey's Court, Ham, near Richmond. Three boys and three girls made up the Newman family, of which John Henry was the eldest. As the family belonged to the middle class, the children were reared in the typical early nineteenth-century gentility of the era. The portrayal of a gentleman in Newman's own *The Idea of a University* reflects in a large degree the training in refinement and manners characteristic of the social milieu of the Newmans. At the age of eleven, Newman is described by his sister Harriet as a "very philosophical young gentleman," observant and considerate of the needs of others, but as generally somewhat bored by too much socializing—an aspect of his personality due to a sensitivity to blame or to not being liked. A special attachment to his mother was noted, as was evidenced by his constant writing to her when he was away from home and by his meticulous choice of gifts to please her. To his sisters, he always demonstrated a tender sympathy and understanding. He frequently read and explained serious stories to the servants of the house. The young Newman was known for his kindness in judgment, truthfulness to facts, and aversion to childish exaggerations and distortions.[2]

In 1808, Newman's formal education began at a private school in Ealing, where he remained for eight and a half years. All the ingredients necessary for scholarship and leadership became evident in the young schoolboy. George Nicholas, the school's headmaster, has been noted as saying that Newman progressed in his studies at a speed unequaled by any other boy in the school's history.[3] He read constantly, jotting down notes of his readings in a diary which he assiduously kept. He wrote poems, dramas, operas, and for two school papers. He acted in plays, having a special taste for the Roman dramatist, Terence. Only in one area of school life did Newman show little interest. Physically delicate and shy, he refrained from much active participation in sports. But this lack of "rubbing elbows" with his classmates on the athletic field did not cause the boys to classify him as unmanly and to dub the young "bookworm" as unfit to lead, for he was often called upon to serve as an arbitrator in their disputes.[4] Although Newman considered himself as "without a grain of conviviality," [5] thereby frequently remaining aloof from his classmates, he was developing that potential in him for scholarship and leadership which his classmates had already begun to acknowledge.

Throughout his early formative years, Newman was intensely preoccupied with religious reading and thinking, more so than would be expected of a youth at this stage in life. Many of the ideas that he entertained no doubt reflected immaturity of thought; but they nevertheless played an important role in his later theological development and writings, his major contribution.[6] Familiarity with the Bible, which he read with great delight, was the result of his religious training at home. Reared in the Anglican faith, he deemed his knowledge of the Catechism "perfect." [7] He admittedly, however, was not deeply religious in childhood—by which Newman meant that he did not perceive the true meaning of loving God; and he had formed no religious convictions until he was fifteen.[8]

While on vacation in 1820, and again in 1823, he recorded some religious thoughts of his childhood that he felt had a bearing on later convictions. These early notes, later set forth in his *Apologia,* show him as swayed by imagination and superstition. As his imagination "ran on unknown influences, on magical powers, and talismans," he visualized life as a dream, himself as an angel, and all this world as a deception; he even wished that the Arabian Tales were true. He attributed to superstition the practice of making the sign of the cross whenever he entered the dark.[9]

At the age of fourteen, the readings of the precocious Newman led him into mild skepticism about revealed religion—a natural by-product of one who had been influenced by superstition. He took pleasure in reading the objections to revelation contained in Thomas Paine's *Tracts against the Old Testament* and some of David Hume's *Essays,* including the essay on miracles. His reaction to reading the French Deist Voltaire's denial of the immortality of the soul was, "How dreadful, but how plausible." [10]

A year later, at the age of fifteen, any influence that these skeptic authors may have had on Newman's mind vanished. The sermons of and the conversations with the Reverend Walter Mayers of Pembroke College, Oxford, became "the human means" of a "beginning of divine faith" in the young scholar.[11] The baptized Anglican was directed to read the writings of Evangelical divines, Calvinistic in character. From William Romaine, he learned the doctrine of final perseverance and of predestination; from Thomas Scott, an enduring faith in the Holy Trinity and the other fundamentalist dogmas of Christianity and an appreciation of a "bold unworldliness." [12] Thus, the "would-be" skeptic never materialized. The faith of this introspective personality became confirmed in a "mistrust of the reality of material phenomena" and convinced "in the thought of two, and two only, absolute and luminously self-evident beings—myself and my Creator." [13] Reflecting in later life about his brief bout with skepticism, Newman wrote to his friend Edward Pusey in 1845, "I thank God that He shielded me morally from what intellectually might easily come on me—general skepticism." [14]

At the age of fifteen, Newman also read two other books that were to leave an imprint in his mind. Joseph Milner's *History of the Church of Christ* introduced him into the study of the Church Fathers, particularly St. Augustine and St. Ambrose; and their influence became notable in his works, *The Arians of the Fourth Century* (1833) and *The Development of Christian Doctrine* (1845). The reading of Thomas Newton's *Dissertations on the Prophecies* was instrumental in convincing him that the Pope was the anti-Christ predicted by Daniel, St. Paul, and St. John—a belief he held until 1843, two years before his conversion to Roman Catholicism.[15]

While Newman had become attracted to the doctrines of Calvinism, he was never wholly influenced by them. The sternness of Calvinism could affect a personality already inclined towards austerity and a deep sense of human sinfulness; but it could not produce a morbidity and moroseness so characteristic of those who believe in the total depravity of human nature. Newman stressed more the idea that he was predestined to election to eternal glory than that others were undoubtedly predestined to eternal death. In a letter to his mother, Newman set forth his feelings towards sin, predestination, and the effect of Calvinism upon him:

If they made me melancholy, morose, austere, distant, reserved, sullen, then indeed they might with justice be the subject of anxiety, but if, as I think is the case, I am always cheerful, if at home I am always ready and eager to join in any merriment, if I am not clouded with sadness, if my meditations make me neither absent in mind nor deficient in action, then my principles may be gazed at and puzzle the gazer, but they cannot be accused of bad practical effects. Take me when I am most foolish at home and extend mirth into childishness; stop me short and ask me then what I think of myself, whether my opinions are less gloomy; no, I think I should seriously return the same answer that I "shudder at myself." [16]

The autumn of 1816 saw still another eventful turn in Newman's mind. He felt that it was God's will for him to lead a single life: a necessity in that he envisioned a life dedicated to missionary work among the heathen; and a logical conclusion in that in his self-absorption he distrusted material reality and preferred to consider himself and God only.[17] These early formative years of John Henry Newman had begun, therefore, to set the stage for future significant decisions in his life: dedication to scholarly pursuits and ordination to the Anglican priesthood.

II *Student at Trinity*

After Newman had completed his course at Ealing, he was undecided as to the choice of either Cambridge or Oxford as the university in which to continue his studies. With his father he sought advice from the Reverend Mr. John Mullins, a curate at

St. James's Church, Piccadilly. As a graduate of Oxford, Mullins favored his alma mater and sought to enroll young Newman in his own college of Exeter. Since no vacancies existed for new students, Trinity College appeared as the next best choice. On December 14, 1816, John was accepted as a commoner of Trinity College, Oxford; but he did not commence studies until the following June.

Oxford in the nineteenth century was still bound to the Church of England, and a prerequisite for admission was formal subscription to the Thirty-nine Articles. With tutors who were ordained clergymen of the Established Church, the elements of theology were systematically presented. Based on the medieval plan of higher education, Oxford was a colony of twenty independent colleges. The curriculum reflected the medieval ideal: modern philosophy was not taught, but only the philosophical systems of Plato and Aristotle; modern history had no place in its curriculum, as the ancient histories of Greece and Rome—written by Herodotus, Thucydides, Livy, and Tacitus—were read; Latin and Greek were the only languages studied; and although some mathematics was included, natural science received no attention. Curricularly, Oxford at the beginning of the nineteenth century may well be said to have been living in an ancient past, within a medieval framework.[18]

As for the students at Oxford, the majority appeared to be attending college for the sole purpose of fulfilling a social and traditional obligation to their family class. In the absence of serious interest in studies, wine parties of a riotous nature became the favorite pastime of the students and even of the heads of student houses. Newman the young scholar objected vigorously to this orgiastic way of life: he would not take part in their parties. Although at first resented by his fellow students for remaining socially aloof, he later gained their respect.[19] Moreover, the intellectual idleness and licentiousness of Oxford began to draw attention. The *Edinburgh Review* from 1808 to 1810 attacked the situation at the university, and the results were the selection of administrators and tutors more capable of providing an atmosphere conducive to keener intellectual activity.[20]

In the midst of an intellectual renewal at Oxford, Newman pursued his scholarly goals with serious intensity. He was known to read from eight to twelve hours a day; and his tutor, Mr.

Thomas Short, could hardly keep pace with suggestions for the omnivorous reader. Young Newman was, therefore, allowed to plan his own reading program. The serious study won for him a substantial scholarship for future years of study, and he was elected in 1818 a scholar of Trinity.[21]

During the vacation of 1818, Newman delved into the writings of the historian Edward Gibbon and the philosopher John Locke. He became enamored of Gibbon's style and ideas. "My ears rang with the cadence of his sentences," he wrote to a friend; and Newman rendered an analysis of the Greek historian Thucydides in Gibbon's style.[22] Although he was fully aware of Gibbon's skepticism towards Christianity, Newman admired his ability as a historian and regarded him as the only English writer that could be called an ecclesiastical historian. Concerning Gibbon's treatment of the "Five Causes of Christianity," Newman did not deny them; he merely considered them as "not sufficient." [23] Newman made no comment on Locke's influence upon him at this time; but, in later writings, as in his *Grammar of Assent,* he reflects a Lockean approach to the theory of knowledge.

While at Trinity, Newman began one of his closest friendships, with John William Bowden—a friendship that lasted until Bowden's death in 1844. Born on the same day but three years apart —Newman was sixteen; Bowden, nineteen—the two students became "inseparables, reading, walking and boating together." [24] In 1819, Newman and Bowden collaborated in producing a periodical, *The Undergraduate.* The short-lived endeavor, of several issues only, contained principally comic verses. Since the publicity resulting from the publication centered solely upon himself, it led the bashful Newman to withdraw from the venture; he also wanted due recognition for Bowden. The two young Oxford scholars also joined efforts in issuing a two-part poem, "St. Bartholomew's Eve" in the same year. The poem described the unfortunate, clandestine marriage of a Protestant gentleman and a Roman Catholic lady, and both of whom die tragically because of the machinations of a cruel and fanatic priest. The poem was a jestful condemnation of the St. Bartholomew's Day massacre which had occurred in France in 1572 and in which thousands of Huguenots were killed.[25]

A career in law was the intended goal for Newman at this time—a career most acceptable to his father as it would prepare his son for entrance into political life. Young Newman, however, became disturbed at being "too solicitous about fame" and expressed "dismay" at such "high expectations." "I fear much more from failure," he commented, "than I hope from success." [26] And in 1820 it was failure that confronted the promising young scholar. In attempting to maintain a daily schedule of as many as twelve to fifteen hours of serious study and reading, Newman broke down in exhaustion from strain and overwork. Besides, he felt the loss of the companionship of his close friend Bowden, who had now assumed studies for law in London, and he was preoccupied with the possible bankruptcy of a brewhouse recently acquired by his father. Having been called a day earlier to his examination only intensified his nervous condition, and he found himself unable even to complete the examination. Classmates anticipated his winning honors; Newman ended up in failure.

Newman, however, embraced defeat with fortitude; for, as he wrote his father, "I have done everything I could to attain my object; I have spared no labour and my reputation in my college is as solid as before if not as splendid." [27] He decided to continue at Trinity since his previously earned scholarship was still available; but he agreed with his father's advice that a legal and political career, with the attendant uncertainties and tensions inherent in it, should be discarded. Newman's scholarly inclinations towards church history and theology and his preference for religious over worldly tastes could easily lead him now to decide in favor of a career in Holy Orders.[28]

With a new goal in view and with a better understanding of the reasons for his previous failure, the resilient Newman continued his studies at Trinity. He wanted to atone for his failure with success even though he realized that to do so fed his ambitious pride. When he coveted a fellowship at Oriel College, an institution known for having the most engaging intellectuals at Oxford, he reproached himself: "I deprecate the day in which God gives me repute or any approach to wealth. . . . I am praying to get into Oriel and to obtain the prize for my essay." [29] "To live and die a Fellow of Oriel" became his all-absorbing desire; and he spared no effort; he knew how to pace himself in study and in readings.[30] From April 6 to 11, 1822, he took the required examinations; on April 12, the news of election reached him. He at first accepted the announcement nonchalantly and continued to

play the violin—he had learned to play in childhood; but, after a few moments of reflection, he "flung down his instrument and dashed downstairs with all speed to Oriel College." [31]

Newman reacted to the congratulations with all the enthusiasm of a youth of twenty-one. In a triumphant tone he wrote to his father, "I am absolutely a Member of the Common Room." [32] Humility, a virtue not readily found in youth, gave way at least for the moment to all the doors of ambition that this newly won distinction could open up.

III   Fellow at Oriel

At Oriel the young scholar lived in an atmosphere conducive to his religious tastes and one that challenged an intellect already keen and active. He took to the "high and broad platform of University society and intelligence" offered at Oriel.[33] The pride that had engulfed him on his first day as he found himself, with awe, among the "greats" of Oxford's students and teachers soon turned into humble self-consciousness; indeed, he found it so difficult to express himself freely with them that he was suspected of being a stutterer.[34] As his earlier shyness became intensified, he questioned his worthiness of being elected to such an honor. He considered his earlier Calvinistic belief a drawback, responsible for narrowness and even "real isolation of thought and spiritual solitariness." [35]

As Newman cherished his Oriel status and was determined to profit from it, he discovered in Richard Whately his first principal influence at Oriel—an influence that transformed the raw, bashful youth into an independent and brilliant thinker. In 1825, Newman wrote to Whately, "Much as I owe to Oriel in the way of mental improvement, to none, as I think, do I owe so much as to you." [36] Whately directed Newman to the trend towards the liberal theology being expounded at Oriel in the 1820s. The leaders of this trend were known as Noetics because "they called everything into question; they appealed to first principles, and disallowed authority as a judge in intellectual matters." [37] Whately impressed on Newman the idea of the church as "a substantial body or corporation," which by its nature must stand independent of the state. The church ought not have any right to interfere in temporal affairs; and the state, in spiritual ones. With other theological tenets of Whately, however, Newman found little or no sympathy.[38]

Edward Hawkins, Provost of Oriel and Vicar of St. Mary's, was another influence on Newman. The reading at Hawkins' suggestion of Sumner's *Treatise on Apostolical Teaching* led Newman to forsake whatever vestige of Calvinism remained in him and to accept the doctrine of regeneration through baptism: mankind was no longer subject to the procrustean bed of being either saved or unsaved. The value of tradition in religious belief had a greater effect on Newman's thinking; for, by this doctrine, the Christian faith was a body of teachings handed down from one generation to another. The role of Scripture, thereby, was not primarily to teach doctrine but to prove it. For a more complete view of Christianity, one must have recourse to the Creeds and to the other official documents that the church has issued to set forth more clearly the teachings of Christ.[39]

While under the influence of the Noetics from 1822 to 1827, Newman read in 1823 Bishop Butler's *Analogy of Religion* and became more convinced of the need of a philosophical basis for religion. As a result, Newman acquired a better appreciation of revelation as a guide to understanding the world and also of the necessary limitations of human knowledge for interpreting matters of religion, thus demonstrating the "logical cogency of faith." [40] In drifting towards the liberal views of the Noetics, he began "to prefer intellectual excellence to moral";[41] but illness and bereavement encouraged a reexamination of his liberal views. When nervous exhaustion again overtook him in November, 1827, the Noetic view of religion on a sheer intellectual level left Newman unsustained. But his sister Mary's death at the age of nineteen in January, 1828, was a more significant influence; for the two had always been close and had frequently corresponded. Her image was ever before him; and in May, 1828, he wrote to his sister Jemima: "I wish it were possible for words to put down those indefinite, vague, and withal subtle feelings which pierce the soul and make it sick. Dear Mary seems embodied in every tree and hid behind every hill. What a veil and curtain this world of sense is!" [42] The reality of the unseen world overpowered Newman—a world nonexistent for the ever-questioning liberal. When Newman had examined his views, he found that the heart, as well as the mind, has a place in religion: "It is so difficult to realise what one believes, and to make these trials, as they are intended, real blessings." [43]

Meanwhile, Newman had been ordained a deacon in the Anglican Church on June 13, 1824; and he had accepted the position of curate at St. Clement's Church. The following year, on May 29, he was ordained to the Anglican priesthood. In 1825-6, he assisted Whately as vice-principal of Alban Hall. He resigned as curate at St. Clement's upon appointment as one of the public tutors of Oriel in 1826. During the academic years 1827-8, he held the university office of Public Examiner in Classics for the Bachelor of Arts degree. In 1828, he was made vicar of St. Mary's Church, a post he held until 1843; but he continued as Fellow of Oriel until 1845.

IV   The Beginnings of Leadership

The youthful Newman, who had looked upon himself as "abashed and unworthy" to shake the hands of his learned professors and fellow scholars at Oriel and who had remained silently preoccupied with his studies, was ready for leadership. Newman himself noted this transition: "Things changed in 1826. At that time I became one of the Tutors of my College, and this gave me position." Essays which he had written were well received, and he added, "I began to be known. I preached my first University Sermon. . . . It was to me like the feeling of spring weather after winter; and, if I may so speak, I came out of my shell." [44] Samuel Rickards, a friend and fellow Anglican priest, for whom Newman substituted during a vacation, had predicted this transformation from the silent scholar to the leader: "Here is a fellow who, when he is silent, will never begin to speak; and when he once begins to speak, will never stop." [45]

As Newman gained in self-assurance, he began to espouse causes not consonant with two Noetics for whom he had much admiration: Hawkins and Whately. Experience gained as a counselor and comforter of souls at St. Clement's and at St. Mary's gave Newman an apostolic zeal and a religious understanding which he wished to impart to his students at Oriel. He viewed the position of a tutor as a quasi-pastoral function; and, when Oriel's provost, Dr. Hawkins, disagreed, Newman and two fellow tutors, Richard Hurrell Froude and Robert Isaac Wilberforce, were adamant in their stand. They wanted to cultivate special friendships with the most promising students and to see in their charges the opportunity of developing them not only intellectually but also spiritually. Hawkins, who objected vehemently, viewed tutors as merely general lecturers; and, using his authority, he assigned no new students to Newman and the other rebellious tutors. This break with Hawkins occurred in 1829, and Newman was left by the end of 1830 without pupils at Oriel and could not exercise the role he cherished of teaching and of taking pastoral care of young scholars.[46] Freed from teaching duties, Newman now found time to initiate an avid, systematic study of the Church Fathers—a study that altered much of his future thought and writing.

In 1829, Newman made his open disavowal of liberal tendencies in the Anglican Church. The occasion was the Catholic Emancipation Act; the opponent, Dr. Whately, his former mentor. Newman had no special sympathy for or against the act which made it possible for Roman Catholics to vote, to sit in Parliament, and to hold most civil and military offices.[47] Robert Peel, the prime minister, had advocated this bill and had called upon the liberal intellectual leaders of both Oxford and Cambridge for support. Whately, who obliged, became the leader of the Oxford intellectuals in advocating this liberal measure. Newman, who rallied about him those supporting the conservative views of the High Church, stressed the corroding influence of indifferentism in this toleration of papists and accused the political leaders of interference with the church's university.

When Peel ran for reelection, Newman led the members of the Oxford community in a vigorous opposition to him. When Peel's party was defeated for control of Parliament, Newman wrote to his mother, "We have achieved a glorious victory; it is the first public event I have been concerned in, and I thank God from my heart both for my cause and its success. We have proved the independence of the Church and of Oxford. . . . We had the influence of government in unrelenting activity against us and the talent so-called of the University."[48]

Whately, who became disgusted with Newman for heading what was termed "the party of stupidity and intolerance," attributed Newman's defection from liberalism not to conviction but to the ambition of heading his own group of followers.

Writing in retrospect, Newman answered this accusation in the *Apologia* by claiming that it was not he who sought followers but rather it was they who sought him for leadership in this cause.[49] Newman and liberalism had parted company. Enlightened by the experience of over thirty years, Newman rendered a more extensive explanation of the meaning of liberalism in 1864 as a note in his autobiography. He felt the explanation necessary since such outstanding writers and defenders of Roman Catholicism—of which he later became a convert—as Count Montalembert and Father Lacordaire regarded themselves as liberals. To Newman, liberalism meant "false liberty of thought"; he would strongly adhere to open discussion of religious doctrine, if it would not degenerate into a false liberty: "Liberalism then is the mistake of subjecting to human judgment those revealed doctrines which are in their nature beyond and independent of it, and of claiming to determine on intrinsic grounds the truth and value of propositions which rest for their reception simply on the external authority of the Divine Word." [50]

Moreover, the liberalism with which Newman found no favor was that affecting many teachers and students at Oxford: a liberalism tainted with rationalism, it was an "anti-dogmatic spirit" swayed by the "pride of reason." [51] In discussing Thomas Erskine's *Internal Evidence for the Truth of Revealed Religion*, Newman indicated the difficulty of rationalism in viewing revelation as objective truth and the classifying it instead as a product of superstitious minds.[52] In other matters, including religious ones, Newman espoused liberal views and causes; for he strongly defended an individual's freedom of conscience, the role of personal experience in the development of religious belief, the independence of the church from the state, wider participation of laymen in church affairs, and a lessening of the bureaucratic structures of the church. As Charles Sarolea has concluded, "Newman was a liberal Catholic in the highest sense of the word." [53]

V   The Arians of the Fourth Century

When the task of studying the Church Fathers became Newman's primary concern after he was left without students to tutor, he quickly seized upon the invitation to participate in a projected ecclesiastical history and agreed to write a serious work entitled *The Arians of the Fourth Century*. "I have nothing to say except that my work opens a grand and most interesting field to me," he commented while engrossed in the subject.[54] The Fathers appealed to him not only through their doctrine but also through their humanity: they "do not put away their natural endowments, but use them to the glory of the Giver. . . . They are versed in human knowledge; they are busy in human society; they understand the human heart. . . . Thus they have the thoughts, feelings, frames of mind, attractions, antipathies of other men, . . . only they have these properties of human nature purified, sanctified, and exalted." [55]

The Council of Nicaea, held in the year 325, was Newman's assigned subject. The council had dealt with the doctrine of the Trinity and had issued a formal statement of faith, the Nicene Creed, which asserted Christ's coeternity and consubstantiality with God the Father. But Newman, who became absorbed in the development of the Arian party which had denied the eternal coexistence of Christ with the Father, became so particularly attracted to Athanasius of Alexandria, the stalwart champion of the Trinity against the Arians, that the work and proceedings of the council received only a scant summary at the end of his book. Upon hearing of such a lengthy exposition on Athanasius and the Arians, his friend Froude wrote of his concern as to whether or not the assigned subject would ever be duly considered. Newman replied: "Recollect, my good sir, that every thought I think *is* thought, and every word I write *is* writing, and that thought tells, and that words take room, and that though I make the introduction the *whole* book, yet a book it is." [56] Since the editors of the series did not think that Newman dealt adequately with the assigned topic, the book was not included in the series. Although completed in 1832, it was left to Newman himself to publish the work in 1833. But he was happy to have devoted himself to so intriguing a subject and personality as Athanasius —and happier indeed would he have been to know that he himself has been called "an Alexandrian Greek," "a Greek of Alexandria, . . . mystical, ascetic, uncompromising." [57]

The Arians represented a thorough analysis of all the conflicting theories about the doctrine of the Trinity prior to the Council of Nicaea. Each theory was studied in itself and as it contributed to the position of the Arians in the fourth century. The texts of Sacred Scripture dealing with the Trinity in the Old and New

Testaments were examined; the writings of the Fathers and the early documents of the church were studied and compared to clarify inconsistencies arising out of variations of philosophical terms employed; and Newman offered a brilliant defense of the church's obligation to formulate Creeds and to decide upon disputed interpretations of religious doctrine. Scripture by its very nature, he claimed, was unsystematic and required a system of doctrine; therefore, "being framed, let it be observed, not with a view of explaining, but of arranging the inspired notices concerning the Supreme Being, of providing, not a consistent, but a connected statement." [58] As society, the more complex it becomes, must continuously examine its code of laws in the light of changing situations, so the church must be aware of the corrupting influence of heresy. Misinterpretation of Sacred Scripture, unless clarified by church Creeds, could cast serious doubt and confusion as to belief and worship of God. "If the Church would be vigorous and influential it must be decided and plain-spoken in its doctrine." [59]

In this scholarly work Newman produced a definitive study of the Arians and ante-Nicene teachings about the Trinity. Students of Newman, however, have not been exuberant in their praise of it. Charles F. Harrold feels that the study was a disappointment even to Newman's friends, for "the historical passages are colorless," and the chronology at times becomes "ignored or confused." Although regarded as scholarly, it is an unexciting, highly complicated theological exposition, one laboriously written and full of details.[60] Jean Guitton, though singling it out as an excellent indication of Newman's thought as it was shaping itself, listed it as "a dull book to most readers." [61]

VI   *Mediterranean Tour*

In writing *The Arians,* Newman frequently worked himself to the point of exhaustion; its completion necessitated a period of relaxation.[62] An invitation from his friend Froude, who also needed a vacation to restore his health, to a Mediterranean tour appeared welcome; and in December, 1832, the two friends set sail.[63] Newman became enchanted with the places he saw and visited: the sees of the Fathers of the Church, the stops of St. Paul's missionary journeys, the sites of Carthage and the Punic Wars. The misery and poverty of Sicily, however, saddened him.

He admired the beauty of Amalfi and Salerno; but Naples, despite its natural beauty, he termed a "watering-place amidst lumpish hills like bolsters." He stood on Mount Vesuvius and visited the excavations at Pompeii and Herculaneum.[64] Ancient and Christian Rome made a lasting impression on him; yet he still called Rome "a city under a curse" and expressed the hope, "O that thy creed were sound!" He even wrote home, "as to the *Roman* Catholic system, I have ever detested it so much that I cannot detest it more by seeing it." [65] However, Newman later admitted that his judgment was not based on any intimate knowledge of Roman Catholics and their religion.[66]

Although Newman was apparently absorbed in the beauty and wonder of the Mediterranean world, his heart and mind never really left his native England: "England was in my thoughts solely, and the news from England came rarely and imperfectly." [67] Two concerns appeared uppermost in his mind about England: the future of the Church of England and that of himself. Even before embarking for the Mediterranean journey, the liberal party was aiming at the disestablishment of the Anglican Church. A bill for the suppression of the Irish sees was being discussed in Parliament. Newman consequently "had fierce thoughts against the Liberals" and the possibility of their success "fretted" him inwardly.[68]

The moments of relaxation and quiet solitude, as he and Froude did not always travel together, encouraged Newman to record his thoughts in verses which reflected his unsettled state of mind and his preoccupation with the future. Their titles confirm this theme: "Temptation," "Absolution," "Private Judgment," "The Watchman," "Penance," "Desolation," "Our Future." To great leaders in the Bible he looked for inspiration: Moses, Jeremiah, Abraham, Melchizedek, David, Isaac, Jonathan, Jonah, St. Paul. But Newman had hope in the ultimate triumph of the church and of the cause of truth. Off the coast of Algiers on December 20, 1832, he wrote "The Patient Church." [69] And while on the island of Malta he wrote on December 24, 1832, "The Course of Truth." [70]

From December to February, while Newman was at sea, he composed verses almost every day. He wrote them for the *British Magazine,* but many of them were later included in the volume *Lyra Apostolica* (1836), which included poems written by five of his associates in the Oxford Movement: Froude, Keble, Bowden, Wilberforce, and Williams. The verses expressed in poetic form the aspirations and sentiments of that movement. Concerning Newman's poems, Hutton has written: "For grandeur of outline, purity of taste and radiance of total effect, I know hardly any short poems in the language that equal them." [71]

Newman did not always attain the rest and relaxation desired from his Mediterranean tour: traveling exhausted him and several illnesses afflicted him. In Sicily, the most severe of these illnesses occurred. A fever lasting three weeks even seemed to presage death; and he dictated instructions to his servant as to what should be done if he died. But Newman stubbornly repeated, "I shall not die. . . . I have a work to do in England." [72] He felt destined by God to lead a great work, but he feared that it was his pride that judged him a great man. He wrote home of this inward struggle:

I felt and kept saying to myself "I have not sinned against light," and at one time I had a most consoling, overpowering thought of God's electing love, and seemed to feel I was His. But I believe all my feelings, painful and pleasant, were heightened by somewhat of delirium, though they still are from God in the way of Providence. Next day the self-reproaching feelings increased. I seemed to see more my utter hollowness. . . . Indeed, this is how I look on myself; very much, (as the illustration goes) as a pane of glass, which transmits heat, being cold itself. I have a vivid perception of the consequences of certain admitted principles, have a considerable intellectual capacity of drawing them out, have the refinement to admire them, and a rhetorical or historical power to represent them; and, having no great (i.e., no vivid) love of this world, whether riches, honours, or anything else, and some firmness and natural dignity of character, take the profession of them upon me, as I might sing a tune which I liked—loving the Truth, but not possessing it, for I believe myself at heart to be nearly hollow, i.e., with little love, little self-denial. I believe I have some faith, that is all; and as to my sins, they need my possessing no little amount of faith to set against them and gain their remission. [73]

This self-appraisal admitting human weakness and sin was followed by abandonment to the will of God and to hope in God's Providence for direction of his future: "I had a strange feeling . . . that I must put myself in His path, His way, that I must do my part, and that He met those who rejoiced and worked righteousness, and remembered Him and His ways." [74]

In May, 1833, Newman expressed a longing to return home; but he could not book passage for three weeks. On his homeward voyage many of the thoughts and feelings of his trip began to crystallize, and he synthesized them in the famous poem, "The Pillar of the Cloud," which he wrote on June 16.

> Lead, Kindly Light, amid the encircling gloom
> Lead Thou me on!
> The night is dark, and I am far from home—
> Lead Thou me on! [75]

Newman's soul had undergone a spiritual catharsis. Inspired by the Book of Exodus (13:21)—"And the Lord went before them to show the way by day in a pillar of cloud, and by night in a pillar of fire: that he might be the guide of their journey at both times"—Newman offered a personal confession and statement of faith characteristic of one convinced of a mission to fulfill. On July 9, when he arrived in London, the situation was ripe for a leader; and Newman became that leader.

CHAPTER 2

The Oxford Movement

WHEN Newman returned to England in the summer of 1833, he found evidence justifying his fears for the future of the Anglican Church. The eminent Oxford professor, Thomas Arnold, had written: "The Church, as it now stands, no human power can save." [1] The liberal Whig party was now in power; for generations the Established Church had allied itself with the conservative Tory power. The Anglican bishops, as members of the House of Lords, had offended the common people by voting against the Reform Bill of 1832, which sought the extension of the franchise; the Irish sees had already been suppressed by Parliament; and a group known as the Erastians were attempting to influence the Whigs with the view of Thomas Hobbes that the state, not the church or the Bible, ought to be the final authority about religious belief. Disestablishment of the church was certainly passing from the realm of the possible to the probable.

The Anglican Church itself appeared ineffective in counteracting the tide running against her. Most of the intellectuals belonged to the liberal side. Its clergy "had become, for the most part, amiable and respectable gentlemen, who were satisfied to read Morning and Afternoon Service on a Sunday, and to dislike Dissenters." [2] The bishops, having been appointed by Tory prime ministers for many years, were regarded as agents of a defunct Tory government and were known for their practice of nepotism and political patronage.[3] Moreover, the liberal cause was aided by the liberal spirit rampant on Continental Europe. The French Revolution had canonized liberal secularistic ideas, and the July Revolution of 1830 in France, which Newman regarded as "the triumph of irreligion," [4] had popularized the new watchwords of "progress," "reason," "disestablishment"; Auguste Comte's Positivism challenged the traditional methods of studying God, religion, and society; and German theologians were even employing a new historical methodology that startled everyone in their application of it to the Bible. The desire of workers to share the gains of the Industrial Revolution with capitalists made many more concerned with acquiring the riches of the earth rather than aiming at a heavenly goal. True, there were Romanticists in England who called for an emphasis upon man's spiritual depths instead of upon material satisfaction; but they were weak voices in the wilderness. Thomas Carlyle has aptly termed the period as one "destitute of faith and terrified at skepticism." [5]

I *Beginnings of the Oxford Movement*

On July 14, 1833, five days after Newman's return to England, John Keble preached at Oxford his famous Assis Sermon, published under the title of "National Apostasy." Keble condemned the liberalism of the age and feared that its triumph could divide greatly between one's duties toward the church and the state. He pleaded for "resignation" on the part of devoted members of the church. Although Newman and Froude preferred action, Newman regarded the day as the start of a religious movement.[6] The clarion call was sounded; the Oxford Movement began. As a reform movement within the Church of England, it sought to demonstrate the continuity between the primitive church of the Fathers and the Anglican Church of the nineteenth century and to stem the tide of rationalism and liberalism which could undermine her doctrine and authority.

For the purpose of concerted action, a meeting was held from July 25 to 29. An Association of Friends of the Church was proposed, but only petitions to clergy and laity urging the support of the Established Church emerged. Froude attended the meeting, as did Hugh James Rose, a Cambridge man and editor of the *British Magazine,* which had published Newman's Mediterranean verses; but Newman did not attend, largely because he disliked the valuable time lost at meetings by too much talk and argument. "No great work was done by a system," he later commented on this decision, "whereas systems rise out of individual exertions." [7] When differences as to courses of action arose at the meeting, Newman felt all the more justified in individual effort.

Newman began to make visits and to write letters to clergymen and friends. Whether these were members of the High Church or the Low Church did not matter; his main intent was to unite all who were opposed to the liberal cause. Most of these attempts appeared unsatisfactory to Newman, but he was assured that a trend of popular opinion was slowly turning toward the church. He also inaugurated a series of letters to a newspaper, *The Record,* in which he dealt primarily with church reform and discipline, as based on Scripture and as applied in the context of the day. The series terminated with the sixth letter, which dealt with temperance societies. The editor feared a possible controversy on the topic, which he felt undesirable; and so this other effort came to an end.[8]

Newman, who now saw the need for more deliberate action, issued on September 9, 1833, three tracts, the beginning of a series to which others, notably Froude and Pusey, also contributed and which was published as *Tracts for the Times.* Friends and ex-pupils were enlisted to distribute these leaflets; even the shy Newman engaged in their hand-to-hand distribution; for he was "becoming perfectly ferocious in the cause."[9] Tract 1, a four-page leaflet, was entitled "Thoughts on the Ministerial Commission" and was addressed to the clergy. Writing anonymously, Newman boldly warned: "Should the Government and the country so far forget their God as to cast off the Church, to deprive it of its temporal honours and substance, *on what* will you rest the claim of respect and attention which you make upon your flocks? Hitherto you have been upheld by your birth and education, your wealth, your connexions; should these secular advantages cease, on what must Christ's ministers depend?" Newman answered his own question: "Christ has not left His Church without claim of its own upon the attention of men. . . . Hard Master He cannot be, to bid us oppose the world, yet give us no credentials for so doing." And Newman emphasized the real ground of authority, too often neglected—"our apostolical descent."[10]

A total of ninety tracts were issued from September, 1833, to February, 1841, of which Newman wrote twenty-nine.[11] Every aspect of religion and of the Anglican Church was examined in these leaflets: church government and administration, doctrine, moral teachings, worship, ecclesiastical history. Repeatedly emphasis was laid upon the doctrine of apostolic succession with its basis in Sacred Scripture and in the teachings of the Fathers of the Church. The tracts were always unsigned. With the exception of the "Tract on Baptism" to which Edward B. Pusey added his initials, thus causing the group to become known as the Puseyites. The name of Pusey added prestige to the movement since he was a professor and canon of Christ Church, Oxford. The writers of the tracts were also referred to as Tractarians because of the manner in which they released their views.

Many of the ideas contained in John Keble's *The Christian Year,* published in 1827, were revived in the Tracts. Newman's friendship with Keble had begun in 1828, although he had known him as a student at Oriel and had always admired his reputation as an outstanding scholar. Keble had been the teacher of Froude, who was largely instrumental in having Newman and Keble discuss their common leanings in theology. Newman's belief in the importance of authority in religious matters, an appreciation of the sacramental system as "the doctrine that material phenomena are both types and the instruments of real things unseen," and his new insight into Butler's doctrine of probability as "living power of faith and love" are attributed to Keble's influence.[12]

In 1836, Newman began to edit an English translation of patristic writings to be known as the "Library of the Fathers." He also became editor of the *British Critic,* which became the official organ of the Oxford Movement. With Pusey, Newman led in that same year a successful fight against the appointment of Renn Dickson Hampden as a professor at Oxford. Hampden, a liberal, was appointed by the Whig government; but opposition was so great that a committee was formed to investigate Hampden. Newman and Pusey, assigned to the committee, convinced its members to reject the appointment of Hampden—a victory for the conservative Oxford group.

The power of the pulpit was also a powerful force that Newman employed during the Tractarian days. His famous four o'clock Sunday afternoon sermons at St. Mary's, Oxford, drew crowds. His sermons, not marked by elaborate argumentation, were "plain, direct, unornamented, clothed in English that was only pure and lucid, free from any faults of taste, strong in their flexibility and perfect command, . . . in their piercing and large insight into character." [13] He did not repeat views in the *Tracts* but chose a wide range of topics: "The Individuality of the Soul," "The Invisible World," "The Ventures of Faith," "Warfare the Condition of Victory," "The Cross of Christ the Measure of the World," "The Church a Home for the Lonely." His appeal was primarily to the heart and not to the mind. "After hearing these sermons," observed a listener, "you might come away still not believing the tenets peculiar to the High Church system; but you would be harder than most men, if you did not feel more than ever ashamed of coarseness, selfishness, worldliness, if you did not feel the things of faith brought closer to the soul." As a result, even "those who by early education and conviction were kept aloof from the peculiar tenets of High Churchmen could not but acknowledge the moral quickening which resulted from the movement, and the marvelous character of him who was the soul of it." [14] When published, these sermons "put all other sermons out of the market." [15]

II   *The* Via Media

While Newman wrote his tracts, preached his sermons, and delved more thoroughly into the Church Fathers for a vision of the primitive church, he began the formulation of a theory called the *Via Media*. Opponents of the Oxford Movement charged it with "Popery" and declared that it would eventually lead to Roman Catholicism. To disavow such a leaning, Newman responded in lectures delivered at St. Mary's; and these he later recast for publication in 1837 as *The Prophetical Office of the Church, Viewed Relatively to Romanism and Popular Protestantism;*[16] and in this work his *Via Media* theory first appeared. Since the title seemed negative, he felt it necessary to give definite shape and character to the content. Newman enumerated the many points of agreement between the Anglican Church and the Roman Church; indeed, he insisted that the Catholic Church in all lands had been one from the first for many centuries. But, in the course of time, Rome had made many superstitious additions to the original body of divine truths; Protestantism, on the other hand, had capriciously subtracted. The Anglican Church stood in the safe, middle way between these extreme positions; it had remained faithful to the original apostolic church; and its presentation of unblemished divine truth throughout the centuries made it the true church.

More specifically, in *The Prophetical Office* Newman dealt with the problem of religious authority. Roman Catholicism, he argued, went to one extreme in her doctrine of infallibility by often neglecting and even overriding the consent of the Fathers as necessary historical evidence for belief: "We have her own avowal that the Fathers ought to be followed, and again that she does not follow them." [17] Furthermore, Newman also noted a contradiction in the notion of infallibility and the limitations of human knowledge. Protestantism went to the extreme of private judgment, which Newman characterized as an absurdity since man always needed to rely on some form of authority and rarely ever acted solely on private judgment.[18] The Anglican Church, in opposition to these extremes, pursued a *via media* between authoritarianism and anarchic individualism, thereby conforming to the early church, which claimed authority but not infallibility. Thus, the Anglican Church promoted a spirit of intellectual freedom without encroachment upon the mind; yet it curbed that freedom when a tendency to lose restraint arose. Newman had not discarded his earlier view of the Pope as anti-Christ; however, despite many unacceptable doctrines, the Roman Church still maintained a connection with the ancient church. But he saw no hope as yet for his union with or submission to Rome.

Lectures on Justification, published in 1838, sought to find a middle way between Roman Catholics and Lutherans on the topic of worthiness for salvation.[19] The Catholics emphasized a mingling of faith and love that resulted in "good works." The Lutherans held to justification by the power of faith alone; no form of good works or penance would be needed. Roman Catholics placed too much reliance on man's actions; Lutherans, on God. Newman upheld justification by baptism, which elevates man from a state of nature to a state of grace and which thereby opens to man a supernatural faith and gives him power to act meritoriously.[20]

An article, "Prospects of the Anglican Church," in the *British Critic* of April, 1839, showed another development of Newman's *Via Media*.[21] After presenting a résumé of the efforts of the Tractarians to 1839 and after classifying their movement more as a "spirit afloat" reacting to the dry and superficial character of religious teaching and literature and clamoring for a deeper religious philosophy, Newman presented his alternatives: either the *Via Media* of Anglicanism or Roman Catholicism. In his *Lectures on Justification,* he concluded that Luther had placed "Christians in bondage to their works and observances; released them by his doctrine of faith; and left them in bondage to their feelings." [22] Now, he concluded, "The spirit of Luther is dead; but Hildebrand

and Loyola are alive." With the extreme position of Protestantism rejected, Newman asked: "Would you rather have your sons and daughters members of the Church of England or the Church of Rome?" [23]

While this question was still in his mind, Newman continued his study of the early church. His special topic was now the Monophysite or Eutychian heresy. Eutyches[24] had rejected the teaching of the Council of Chalcedon in 451 that Christ possessed both a divine and a human nature; he and his followers, called Monophysites, claimed only a divine nature for Christ and considered his humanity as only an appearance. In studying the different factions of this controversy over Christ's nature, Newman noted a similarity of the *via media* position of the Anglican Church in the nineteenth century to that of the Monophysites of the fifth century. Both argued from the Fathers of the Church and were supported by civil powers; and the *via media* of the fifth century was a heretical position. This led Newman to ponder: "My stronghold was Antiquity; now here, in the middle of the fifth century, I found, as it seemed to me, Christendom of the sixteenth and the nineteenth centuries reflected. I saw my face in that mirror, and I was a Monophysite. The Church of the *Via Media* was in the position of the Oriental Communion, Rome was where she now is; and Protestants were the Eutychians." [25] The tenability of Anglicanism now came into doubt.

Before even concluding his study of the Monophysites, a friend, Robert Williams, drew Newman's attention to an article entitled "Anglican Claim" in the *Dublin Review* by Nicholas Wiseman, a Roman Catholic. Wiseman contended that the Donatists of the fourth century and the Anglicans maintained similar positions. Donatism fell into schism by refusing submission to the authority of the Pope. A quotation of St. Augustine as applied to the Donatists impressed Newman: *Securus judicat orbis terrarum,* "the whole world judges right." Donatism then and Anglicanism now stand against the whole church. "By those great words of the ancient Father, interpreting and summing up the long and varied course of ecclesiastical history," Newman later wrote, "the theory of the *Via Media* was absolutely pulverized." [26]

III   *Indecision and Doubt*

But Newman was still in no position to embrace the Church of Rome. In the *British Critic* of January, 1840, he conceded that Rome had the strong point of universality; the Church of England, however, had "primitiveness," since Rome had made many additions to the apostolic faith. "While Rome, though not deferring to the Fathers, recognizes them, and England, not deferring to the large body of the Church, recognizes it, both Rome and England have a point to clear up." [27] Later, he wrote more strongly: "If the Note of schism, on the one hand, lies against England, an antagonist disgrace lies upon Rome, the Note of idolatry." The duty of Anglicans, he felt, was to initiate ways of "how to comport themselves towards the Church of Rome, while she is what she is." [28]

With an ardent concern to free the Anglican Church from the condemnation of schism and to demonstrate her unyielding loyalty to the original apostolic church, Newman threw himself into a study of the Thirty-nine Articles drawn up by the Church of England in the sixteenth century. He concentrated on what appeared to him as the all-conclusive problem: how can the Church of England win back its "Catholic" character? The answer to this question was found in "Remarks on Certain Passages in the Thirty-nine Articles" (Tract 90).

Many Anglicans conceded that their Creeds and *Book of Common Prayer* were capable of a Roman Catholic interpretation— but not the Articles, which were distinctly Protestant. Newman, who wished to extend a Roman Catholic interpretation to the Articles, argued that the Articles were not directed to the teachings of the early church and to the formal dogmas of the Roman Catholic Church as set forth in her general councils, including the Council of Trent in the sixteenth century, which had preceded the formulation of the Articles. But the Articles did condemn many popular beliefs and usages which steadily had crept in through the centuries and which Rome did sanction; these he termed "dominant errors." The Articles were also directed against the political supremacy of the Pope and not against the Church of Rome; and Newman found nothing in apostolic teaching which granted the Pope authority over the whole church. He did concede, however, that, although the

Pope's supremacy was not a matter of faith, it was an expedient ecclesiastical arrangement and a long-standing custom. The Oath of Supremacy enjoined on Englishmen by Henry VIII prevented a foreign prelate from having jurisdiction on anyone in England. Anglicans, therefore, freed themselves only from the Pope's jurisdiction but not from the Church Catholic. "We find ourselves, as a Church, under the King now, and we obey him; we were under the Pope formerly, and we obeyed him." [29] Newman thus felt that he had absolved the Anglican Church of schism and had demonstrated her "Catholic" character.

Tract 90 had been issued on February 27, 1841. Without seeking any defense or explanation from Newman, protests and demonstrations were made in the halls and classrooms of Oxford and from the pulpits of the Anglican Church. Throughout England, Newman was denounced as a traitor to the Church of England and as an advocate of popery and Romanism. He betrayed his allegiance to the Articles which he had sworn to uphold when he had entered Oxford as a student and when he had been ordained to the Anglican ministry. Feelings of mistrust grew. Tract 90 was branded as "evasive hypocrisy," and one prominent churchman's remark was often quoted: "I should be sorry to trust the author of that Tract with my purse." [30] Newman had failed, therefore, to convince his fellow Anglicans; he was not able to have them follow the continuity of his own logic as it had been unfolding itself since the beginning of the Oxford Movement. In the eyes of many in England, he was "a subtle-minded ecclesiastical hairsplitter and special pleader." [31] Anglicans of the twentieth century, reflecting earlier opinion, have labeled Tract 90 as "a very melancholy document" with "a certain double dealing," showing "how a really great man can become little in a false and ambiguous situation," [32] and as a "culmination of sophistries" which "falsify history." [33]

At first, Newman reacted quite calmly to the charges made against him, or almost as if he had anticipated the stir. In a letter to his friend Bowden, he wrote: "Do not think all this will pain me. You see no *doctrine* is censured, and my shoulders shall manage to bear the charge. If you knew all, or when you know, you will see that I have asserted a great principle, and I ought to suffer for it." [34] And to a former pupil, Frederick Rogers, he wrote: "I am now in my right place, which I have long wished to be in, which I did not know how to attain, and which has been brought about without my intention. . . . I cannot anticipate what will be the result of it in this place or elsewhere as regards *myself*. Somehow I do not fear for the *cause*." [35]

Newman, however, underestimated the extent and the depth of opinion against his having written Tract 90. The bishops of the Anglican Church, alarmed by the many protesting letters they were receiving, urged Newman's ecclesiastical superior, Bishop Bagot, to take action. Bagot sought advice from the Archbishop of Canterbury, who deemed desirable the immediate discontinuance of the Tracts. But Newman was requested by Bagot not only to discontinue the Tracts but also to withdraw Tract 90. If Newman had heeded Bagot's decision, his acceptance would have implied that he had received an official censure and that he would have to sacrifice his principles. Newman, caught in an ecclesiastical web, told Pusey that "if it was condemned as to doctrine, I should feel I had no business in his diocese. I should not be signing the articles in the sense he meant them to be signed." [36] Bagot, who respected Newman's position, effected a compromise: Tract 90 would not be censured and could remain in print if Newman discontinued the Tracts and if he would no longer write about the Articles; furthermore, Newman was to send to his bishop a letter, to be made public, stating his repudiation of the Church of Rome.[37] Bishop Bagot accepted the letter as satisfactory since Newman had written: "I think that to belong to the Catholic Church is the first of all privileges here below, as involving in it heavenly privileges, and . . . I consider the Church over which you preside the Catholic Church in this country." [38] For the moment, at least, the turmoil subsided.

Since 1839, Newman had been contemplating the leaving of St. Mary's, Oxford, to live at Littlemore, several miles away, where he had built a church. A number of reasons led to this consideration: he doubted having any pastoral influence over his Oxford parishioners, with whom he admitted having no personal acquaintance; he felt guilty about using St. Mary's as a university office to give prestige to his ideas rather than for the performance of its intended parochial duties; and he also feared that his sermons were disposing the congregation towards Rome. At Keble's advice, however, he decided to continue at St. Mary's; but his trips to Littlemore became more frequent; and, on the publication of

Tract 90 in February, 1841, he was taking steps toward his eventual withdrawal from St. Mary's, Oxford. He spent the summer of 1841 at Littlemore "without any harass or anxiety" on his mind, "determined to put aside controversy," and to translate St. Athanasius.[39]

But anxiety and controversy were Newman's lot. The Anglican bishops, fully aware of the impact of Tract 90, began leveling charges at Newman. A determined movement to discredit him became evident when seven bishops had condemned him by the end of 1841 and twenty-four by 1844. At first, Newman planned a protest; but he felt tied by the cords of ecclesiastical obedience and gave up the thought in despair.[40] On the affair of the Jerusalem bishopric, however, Newman did not give up. A Protestant English bishopric was to be set up in Jerusalem; the bishop was to be consecrated by the Anglican archbishop; and he would rule the Lutheran and Calvinist congregations of the East.

Newman, who considered this act as the granting of status to Protestantism in the East, wrote against the scheme in the July, 1841, issue of the *British Critic;* and he asserted that, while the Anglican Church was censuring him for avowing an approach to the Roman Church, "it actually was courting an intercommunion with Protestant Prussia and the heresy of the Orientals." He also denounced the move as a political stunt of cooperating with the Prussians to offset the influence in Jerusalem of France and Russia, which had established themselves as protectors of the Roman Catholics and of the Orthodox. On November 11, 1841, Newman formally protested to his own bishop and to the Archbishop of Canterbury, but without success; this episode brought Newman "on to the beginning of the end." [41]

In January, 1842, another disappointment followed when John Keble retired from Oxford and his position as Professor of Poetry became vacant. A follower of Newman, Isaac Williams, was considered by many to be the best qualified candidate; but Williams was defeated for the post, presumably on the grounds of his adherence to the Tractarian movement, although he clearly demonstrated no sympathy towards Rome. As an indication of loss of prestige and influence at Oxford, Newman established permanent residence at Littlemore on April 19, 1842. He would minister to his Littlemore parishioners, and his curate to the Oxford members of his congregation. Furthermore, he considered retirement from Oxford expedient in such a period of controversy.

The charges of the Anglican bishops persisted while Newman was at Littlemore. Newspapers circulated all sorts of rumors as to the purpose of his retreat to Littlemore; and "insidious," "sly," "dishonest" were used to describe him. He was even accused of "rearing . . . a nest of Papists." [42] When his attention was called to the descriptions being circulated about Newman and his companions at Littlemore, Bishop Bagot regarded an inquiry necessary; and he requested from Newman an explanation of the reports that he had established an Anglo-Catholic monastery approaching the monastic orders of the Roman Catholic Church. When Newman replied to this and other topics of "incessant interpretation," he denied any erection of a monastery, but he upheld his right to devote himself to a life of greater religious regularity and to more intense personal prayer.[43]

The year 1843 became an eventful one for Newman, for his formal retraction of all he had said against the Church of Rome was published in February in the *Oxford Conservative Journal* with the expected reaction on the part of his opponents; he was branded with the charge of duplicity. In May, Pusey preached a sermon on "The Holy Eucharist a Comfort to the Penitent." Despite Pusey's careful adherence to Anglican doctrine, Oxford's officials suspended him from preaching at the university. Pusey's previous defense of Tract 90 was a sufficient "guilt by association" in the minds of Oxford. In August, the occasion for resigning from St. Mary's took place when William Lockhart, a follower of Newman at Littlemore, joined the Roman Catholic Church and was admitted into one of her monastic orders. When newspapers publicized the conversion and critical letters poured into Littlemore, Newman, convinced that he could no longer maintain a position of leadership and influence while retaining his official post in the Anglican Church, presented his resignation on September 18 as Vicar of St. Mary's to Bishop Bagot.

On September 25, Newman delivered his last sermon as an Anglican, "The Parting of Friends." A hearer noted "the faltering voice, the long pauses, the perceptible and hardly successful efforts at restraining himself, together with the deep interest of the subject which were almost overpowering," as Newman bade farewell to friends, parishioners, and associates at St. Mary's and Oxford.[44] He expressed regret at leaving the church of his birth but, at the same time, found her wanting in adherence to divine truth. He urged everyone present to pray "that in all things he may know God's will, and at all times he may be ready to fulfill it."[45]

Newman retired in quiet seclusion to live a quasi-monastic discipline at Littlemore. Without his leadership, many of his followers became unrestrained in emphasizing the most Roman interpretation of the Oxford Movement; and, by 1845, their influence as a party of reform within the Anglican Church became minimal. Newman's retirement marked an end to any participation on his part in the Oxford Movement.[46] Instead, Newman began a period of intensive prayer and study. Many Anglicans were expecting an immediate announcement of his conversion to Roman Catholicism, but Newman was not yet ready for such a step; his mind was too unsettled. Many followers were looking to him for direction; but his own soul and mind became his only concern. "How could I in any sense," he deliberated, "direct others, who had to be guided in so momentous a matter myself?"[47]

A few of Newman's followers had gone over to the Church of Rome. A year after resigning from the Anglican priesthood, Newman explained the unsettled state of his mind and the difficulty which confronted it in reference to choosing Roman Catholicism:

I had been deceived once; how could I be sure that I was not deceived a second time? I thought myself right then; how was I to be certain that I was now? How many years had I thought myself sure of what I now rejected? how could I ever again have confidence in myself? As in 1840 I listened to the rising doubt in favour of Rome, now I listened to the waning doubt in favour of the Anglican Church. To be certain is to know that one knows; what inward test had I, that I should not change again, after I had become a Catholic? I had still apprehension of this, although I thought a time would come, when it would depart.[48]

Many factors contributed to Newman's hesitation in his acceptance of Roman Catholicism. He would have to forsake the church of his birth, which he had so staunchly defended against the liberals. Many friends and colleagues at Oxford, the associations of many years, would no longer be his. Members of his

family, especially his sisters, noting a possible trend towards
Rome, pleaded with him against taking such a drastic step. He
knew what and whom he was to leave; he did not know what
and whom he was to join. He had had little contact with members of the Roman Catholic clergy and faith. He had been
brought up in a tradition of prejudice towards Roman Catholics,
who, for many years in Great Britain, had been ostracized from
political and social life. He had been to Rome on his Mediterranean trip and remembered her as a "city under a curse." Religious
conversions require more than logic; reason too frequently finds
itself entangled in emotions. Prayer and study were regarded all
the more as necessary means to Newman's searching mind and
soul.

IV   Essay on Development

Towards the end of 1844, Newman resolved to write down the
results of his study at Littlemore in a work that he entitled *An
Essay on the Development of Christian Doctrine*. While review-
ing the thoughts of his projected thesis, he was confronted by
a dilemma of his own making. He had been an exponent of the
static view of the church—a view which held that Christian
truth was known completely by the church at its very beginning
and that, therefore, antiquity was the chief note of the true
church. But he had now become influenced by a more dynamic
view which claimed that, although all truth had been given to
the church upon its establishment, subsequent thought and reflection produces clarification and a better understanding of
Christ's teachings. The fact of heresies, even in early Christianity, proved necessary the action of the church in issuing decrees
of belief for the purpose of avoiding misinterpretation of Christian teaching. Delving farther into the Fathers of the Church and
early Christianity demonstrated to Newman that the growth or
development of Christian doctrine was an idea that clearly existed in theological thought and that St. Irenaeus, Origen, St.
Basil, St. Jerome, and St. Gregory Nazianzen had subscribed at
least implicitly to the view.[49]

In his introduction to the *Essay on Development*, Newman
insisted that Christianity had to be viewed as a historical fact
and that throughout its eighteen hundred years of existence certain apparent inconsistencies and changes in doctrine and wor-

ship have occurred. He regarded any inquiry as to the mode and meaning of these apparent inconsistencies and charges as justified; and, since he himself had been beset by the problem, he directed the *Essay* toward its solution.[50] Concerning the doctrine and worship of Christianity, he mantained that the history of eighteen hundred years ought to make us consider

that the increase and expansion of the Christian Creed and Ritual, and the variations which have attended the process in the case of individual writers and Churches, are the necessary attendants on any philosophy or polity which takes possession of the intellect and heart, and has had any wide or extended dominion; that, from the nature of the human mind, time is necessary for the full comprehension and prefection of great ideas; and that the highest and most wonderful truths, though communicated to the world once for all by inspired teachers, could not be comprehended all at once by the recipients, but, as being received and transmitted by minds not inspired and through media which were human, have required only the longer time and deeper thought for their full elucidation. This may be called *The Theory of Development of Doctrine*.[51]

As Newman sought to substantiate his theory of development, he emphasized the natural function of the human mind as being always engaged in passing judgment on what it comes to know: "We allow nothing to stand by itself: we compare, contrast, abstract, generalize, connect, adjust, classify; and we view all our knowledge in the associations with which these processes have invested it." [52] Such mental activity would not be peculiar to religious ideas alone: mathematical, physical, political, historical, ethical, metaphysical ideas would also be subject to the mind's scrutiny.[53] All ideas characterized as "living" have generated "a general agitation of thought, and an action of mind upon mind." [54] So has been the historical development of such doctrines as "the divine right of kings," "the rights of man," political constitutions, the philosophies of great men.

Since Christianity is a universal religion and is not bound to one locale or period of history, it must be able to accommodate itself towards the world in which it finds itself: its different persons and circumstances of any place or time. All Christian sects have appealed to Scripture, but with varying interpretations of the texts, and even as to the authority to interpret them. The unsystematic structure and figurative style of Scripture have required constant study and examination in the light of changing times—an argument for the development of Christian doctrine as based on Scripture. And Newman emphasized that, "in an age in which reason, as it is called, is the standard of truth and right, it is abundantly evident to any one . . . that, if things are left to themselves, every individual will have his own view of them, and take his own course." [55] To maintain unity and continuity in Christian doctrine throughout all periods of history postulates some supreme power to control the mind and to compel agreement.

By this reasoning Newman concluded in favor of the role of infallibility claimed by the Roman Catholic Church against private interpretation of the Scriptures as advocated by Protestantism: "If Christianity is both social and dogmatic, and intended for all ages, it must humanly speaking have an infallible expounder. Else you will secure unity of form at the loss of unity of doctrine, or unity of doctrine at the loss of form; you will have to choose between comprehension of opinions and a resolution into parties, between latitudinarian and sectarian error." [56] If St. Athanasius or St. Ambrose were to come to life, they would undoubtedly recognize the Roman Catholic Church, and not any other Christian denomination, as the expounder of Christ's doctrine today. Allowance would have to be made for changes of words to explain doctrine; emphasis in argumentation would have to be accommodated to existing circumstances—but these are of the essence of development of doctrine.

Newman had resolved the most pressing difficulty in his mind regarding the acceptance of the Church of Rome: had Rome adhered to or swayed from primitive Christianity? And he concluded that "of all existing systems, the present communion of Rome is the nearest approximation in fact to the Church of the Fathers." [57] Newman, moreover, presented not only a conclusion; he documented it with the results of his serious study in which he contrasted the teachings of Roman Catholicism in the nineteenth century with those of the early Christian Church.

He chose the following doctrines to illustrate a genuine development from earlier and simpler forms: the Canon of the New Testament, the doctrines of Original Sin and Infant Baptism, Communion in One Kind, the Divine Nature of Christ, the In-

carnation, the dignity of the Blessed Virgin and the Saints, and
Papal Supremacy. With proofs taken from the texts of Scripture,
the opinions of Church Fathers, and the practice of the early
church, he demonstrated how these doctrines had developed
throughout the church's history into their form in the nineteenth-
century Church of Rome.[58] Intimate connection and oneness of
past and present in doctrine afforded Roman Catholicism, in
Newman's mind, "undeniably the historical continuation of the
religious system, which bore the name of Catholic in the eight-
eenth century, in the seventeenth, in the sixteenth, and so back
in every preceding century, till we arrive at the first;—undeniably the successor, the representative, the heir of the religion of
Cyprian, Basil, Ambrose, and Augustine. . . . Modern Catholicism is nothing else but simply the legitimate growth and complement, that is, the natural and necessary development, of the
doctrine of the early Church, and that its divine authority is
included in the divinity of Christianity." [59]

But the fact and necessity of development comprise only a
part of Newman's efforts in this treatise; for the process by which
religious ideas genuinely develop forms an even greater section
of his study. In the course of time, an idea may not become a
development; it may become a corruption. Development denotes
life; "corruption, on the contrary, is the breaking up of life, preparing to its termination." [60] Newman distinguishes seven "notes,"
or tests, to judge development or corruption of doctrine. *Preser-
vation of type* is the first test offered, and it is based on the analogy of physical growth. Animals remain within their species
throughout their lives. Birds do not become fish; the child does
not generate into the brute. Continuity of species is maintained.
Ideas also develop with subsequent thought and reflection; they
take on new meaning in the crucible of experience. As Christians
reflected upon and sought to apply Christ's doctrine to their
everyday lives, their faith took on new dimensions without un-
dergoing radical change.[61] Newman details the history of the
church in the first six centuries with all the problems attendant
upon an organization seeking the fullest possible growth in order
to fulfill the aims of its founder. Whether viewed "in its age"
or "in its youth," the organization has maintained identity. In
her growth and development, "such a religion [the Roman Cath-

olic Church] is not unlike the Christianity of the fifth and sixth centuries." [62]

Religious doctrines also evolve from principles. The sciences of mathematics and physics, by analogy, have developed basic permanent principles from which, in the course of study and experimentation, much new knowledge has been derived. Although principles are largely general and abstract, their application leads to the discovery of many new facts. As a second test, *continuity of principles* causes religious doctrine to grow and develop: Christ enunciated the basic permanent principles; His church enlarges upon them as they are applied to future generations.[63] And so the Church of Rome—faithful to Christ's principles, as the supremacy of faith over reason, the preference of the mystical to the literal interpretation of Scripture, the necessity to defend and to transmit defined doctrine—has stood firm, especially against heresies; has maintained the principles and has put them in vigorous operation.[64]

For the third test, *power of assimilation*, Newman again makes use of the analogy of physical growth: life grows by absorbing or assimilating into its own substance external materials, as is done in the matter of food. In the intellectual order, many an idea has resulted from a similar process.[65] In seeking to attract converts, yet desiring to have them feel "at home" in a newly adopted religious faith, the church has frequently employed many customs and usages of pagan rites, such as incense, candles, festival days. Rather than obliterate, the Church has "Christianized" them.[66]

Logical sequence, the fourth test, occasions development simply by affirming any progress of the mind from one judgment to another. If the original teaching is correct, doctrines logically deduced from it represent logical conclusions.[67] To demonstrate this test in the church's history, Newman confines himself to examples of doctrine which consider sin after baptism. The necessity of remitting sin after baptism and of rendering possible reconciliation with God was given serious thought in the early church. In her desire to fulfill Christ's hope for the salvation of sinners and to carry out its authority of "binding and loosing," the church adopted systems of penances and satisfaction for sin.[68]

The fifth test, *anticipation of its future,* considers that an idea that has life has the power to develop under favorable circumstances with the passage of time. The development of a doctrine, therefore, may be vague and slow; but the workings of logical minds will eventually bring a doctrine to its fullest development.[69] Such would be the case, Newman asserts, with doctrines relating to relics, to the cult of saints and angels, and to the Blessed Virgin.[70]

The words of Christ, "I have come not to destroy, but to fulfill," provide the basis for the sixth test: *conservative action upon its past.* Although an idea may have developed with time, "a true development . . . may be described as one which is conservative of the course of antecedent developments being really those antecedents and something besides them: it is an addition which illustrates, not obscures, corroborates, not corrects, the body of thought from which it proceeds."[71] Heresies, Newman points out, have made it necessary for the church to reaffirm previously declared doctrine, as, for example, in the Incarnation, the Trinity, and the Blessed Virgin; but it did so with the purpose of clarification and of placing proper emphasis of various aspects of the specific doctrines.[72]

The seventh and final test is *chronic vigour:* duration or long standing characterizes the faithful development of an idea. Heresies or corruptions of doctrine are short-lived, as are the peculiarities of a country, the customs of a race, or the temporary response to the changing tides of opinion; they cannot maintain their vigor with the passage of time and with divergent cultures.[73] An examination of Roman Catholic doctrines in themselves and in comparison with other religious faiths leads Newman to conclude:

After violent exertion men are exhausted and fall asleep; they awake the same as before, refreshed by the temporary cessation of their activity; and such has been the slumber and such the restoration of the Church. She pauses in her course, and almost suspends her functions; she rises again, and she is herself once more; all things are in their place and ready for action. Doctrine is where it was, and usage, and precedence, and principle, and policy; there may be changes, but they are consolidations or adaptations; all is unequivocal and determinate, with an identity which there is no disputing.[74]

Since Newman presented a developmental theory in 1845, both critics and friends have attributed his view to the influence of nineteenth-century thought.[75] Comte, Condorcet, and Kant viewed humanity as a developing organism; the French Revolution had called for the progressive improvement of mankind, and Hegel had popularized the notion of progress in his philosophy of history. Moreover, Spencer in the field of sociology emphasized the need of man to adjust to a constantly changing environment; indeed, critics have even associated Newman with Darwinian evolution: "We cannot but see on every page of the *Development* Darwin's advancing shadow." [76] Since Newman repeatedly employed the analogy of organic development, his doctrine has been interpreted in biological terms; one critic calls the process of development *epigenesis;* another refers to it as "homogeneous evolution." [77] But the *Origin of the Species* was not published until 1859; and, after its publication, Newman gave no indication of accepting Darwin's thesis in the physiological order, least of all in matters of revealed religion.[78]

Newman had resolved to write the essay on doctrinal development with the purpose of clearing his own mind of the rising doubts in favor of the Roman Catholic Church. At the beginning of writing the essay he acknowledged, "If, at the end of it, my convictions in favour of the Roman Church were not weaker, of taking the necessary steps for admission into her fold." [79] As he progressed in its writing and as his difficulties were gradually resolved, he ceased to speak of "the Roman Catholics"; and he called them "Catholics." "Before I got to the end, I resolved to be received." [80]

Although the essay on doctrine achieved for Newman a justification of the claims of Roman Catholicism, not all Roman Catholics accepted his thesis. Two Jesuit theologians in Rome admitted the principle of development, but they claimed that Newman had carried the principle too far.[81] Newman's American friends wrote of the poor reception of the book by American bishops, who characterized it as "half Catholicism half infidelity." [82] Orestes Brownson, himself a convert, charged Newman with lack of adequate understanding of the Catholic Church and declared that in the essay he reasoned as a Protestant: "This elaborate essay belongs to his past life; let it go with all that Protestantism he abjured before he was permitted to put on the livery of Christ. It belongs not to his Catholic life, and is only accidentally connected with it. . . . The essay he will write hereafter, out of the fulness of his Catholic heart, will breathe a different tone, and fetch another echo." [83] Brownson, who had a static view of Christianity, maintained that the original creed was complete: new definitions of doctrine represented not a subsequent "apprehension and understanding of the sacred deposit of faith committed to her charge" (as Newman asserted), but formulations occasioned by new heresies: "The Church has no natural history, for she is not in the order of nature, but of grace." [84]

Catholic theologians, however, have also indicated that the idea of the development of dogma had existed long before Newman in the writings of the Fathers of the Church and in theological thought.[85] Newman may not have been the originator of the idea, but he has been its ablest expounder. Bishop John J. Wright of Pittsburgh, in speaking of Vatican Council II's role in the updating of Catholic doctrine, echoed Newman's thought: "New Testament verses are the seeds of doctrine. With each popping out of a branch, with each flowering of a leaf, you have a new branch and a new leaf. But each branch and each leaf is in the pattern of the original seed." [86]

V Conversion

Convinced of the truth of Roman Catholicism, Newman's conversion was only a matter of time and circumstance. Two of his companions at Littlemore, Ambrose St. John and John D. Dalgairns, had already joined the Church of Rome. Father Dominic, a missionary in the Congregation of the Passion, planned to visit Dalgairns at Littlemore on October 8, 1845. Newman had submitted his letter of resignation as Fellow of Oriel on October 3, and two days later he noted in his diary that he was making immediate preparation for admittance to Roman Catholicism. With the knowledge of Father Dominic's impending visit, he wrote to Henry Wilberforce that he would ask the missionary priest to receive him into the Church of Rome.[87] On the evening of October 8, Newman was received, with two companions, Frederick Bowles and Richard Stanton.

Upon his conversion Newman's plans for the future were unsettled. Father Dominic suggested that he and his companions visit Bishop Nicholas Wiseman at Oscott and receive the sacrament of confirmation. Newman, who had already met Wiseman as rector of the English College in Rome in 1833, offered Wiseman a copy of his *Essay on Development* for approval. Wiseman felt that the book should be published unchanged or without theological censorship in the hope that it would present a more effective plea for Roman Catholicism. Knowing of the new converts' desire to remain together and also of their unsettled minds as to their next course of action, Wiseman proposed that they move to Old Oscott College in a "Littlemore continued." The converts accepted the offer, and Newman named their house Maryvale.

The secluded life of Littlemore was resumed at Maryvale. Newman declined an offer to write an account of his reasons for joining the Roman Church; he deemed it inopportune to engage in controversy. Moreover, he suggested that the *Essay on Development* had already made his position clear.[88] Instead, Newman preferred to delve into a more thorough study of the ways and traditions of his newly chosen faith and to help his associates prepare for the possible reception of Holy Orders. Although hesitant upon his conversion about being ordained a Roman Catholic priest, Newman decided to take the step. But what work was he to do, and should it be under a bishop of a diocese or in a religious congregation of priests? Father Dominic hoped that the converts would be preachers and missionaries. Bishop Wiseman considered the founding of a school of divinity for preparing future priests—a work for which Newman had had experience as a teacher at Oxford and for which he had demonstrated a wealth of theological knowledge and history in the *Essay on Development*. Since Newman could not make a decision, he expressed the desire to go to Rome and, as his companions felt, have Rome decide for him.[89]

In September, 1846, Newman and St. John left for Rome. They first spent four or five weeks at Milan, where they admired the churches and the art of the city. After a similar study of Rome, they resided at the College of Propaganda, a seminary founded in the seventeenth century for training young men of every nationality for missionary work. When Newman discussed with many in Rome the possibilities of his future work,[90] the objections he heard expressed against his *Essay on Development* dissuaded

him from founding any divinity school. Having a natural bent
towards community life, but for one without too many monastic
restrictions, Newman took a liking for the Oratorians, a congregation founded by St. Philip Neri in the sixteenth century.[91]
Pope Pius IX approved wholeheartedly of Newman's wishes;
and, after Newman's required training period was completed in
Rome, the Pope would concur with the hope of Newman and
the converts to establish themselves as members of this congregation of priests in England.[92] The Pope appointed the Oratorian
Father Carlo Rossi to supervise their training and granted them
the use of a wing of the Monastery of Santa Croce for their home
in Rome. Newman was ordained a Roman Catholic priest on
May 30, 1847.

While in Rome, Newman also found time to write. He directed
his energies to a novel about religious conversion: *Loss and Gain:
the Story of a Convert*, which was published in 1848 upon his
return to England. *Loss and Gain* was occasioned by the success
in England in the summer of 1847 of a novel, whose author was
not identified, *From Oxford to Rome*, which pretended to portray
the inside picture of the "defection" of the Oxford converts to
Roman Catholicism. Newman considered the book as "wantonly
and preposterously fanciful." Rather than honor the book by a
formal critique of its contents, he deemed it more suitable to
answer by writing his novel, one "drawn up with a stricter regard
to truth and probability, and with at least some personal knowledge of Oxford, and some perception of the various aspects of
the religious phenomenon, which the work in question handled
so rudely and so unskilfully." [93]

Newman claimed that *Loss and Gain* was an imaginary tale
and that neither the principal characters nor the history of any
individual mind among the converts was delineated: only "free
use has been made of sayings and doings which were characteristic of the time and place in which the scene is laid." [94] Despite
the unintended suggestion to the reader of real individuals, there
is an obvious identification of the characters in the novel with
Newman's own religious development and experiences at Oxford.
Charles Reding, the main character, bears a striking resemblance
to Newman. Reding, the son of an old-fashioned Anglican clergyman, is sent to Oxford, where he becomes confused as a result
of the conflicting views expressed about religious matters. He

begins to question the Thirty-nine Articles and even becomes interested in Roman Catholicism, to the displeasure of the university authorities. Excessive preoccupation with religious uncertainties causes his failure in his first attempt at examinations. However, since Reding has every desire to remain in the Anglican Church, he spends considerable time reading and studying more about his faith, while also seeking advice from learned Anglican theologians. But these efforts prove fruitless. To the sorrow of family and friends, Reding, who feels in conscience that he must leave the church of his birth, goes to London to be received into the Church of Rome by a Passionist priest.

Reding and Newman, moreover, possessed many of the same personality traits. Both were shy and sensitive, which led to their being misunderstood and to a feeling of isolation. Both were able to overcome their scholastic failure. They were lovers of music, not given over to socializing, and were inclined from youth to a life of celibacy. Both refrained from accepting Roman Catholicism until all reasonable doubt was cleared from their minds.

As a novelist, Newman lacks dramatic quality. The elements of conflict and suspense are superficial since the reader is never held in abeyance as to the next development of the action. In his evaluation of *Loss and Gain,* Baker points out how the novel "reflects merely intellectual steps along the way to conversion, not emotional reaction of man on man." [95] The characters in the novel are classified as "caricatures" and as "shadowy outlines" [96] and as hardly recognizable if met in real life.[97] Yet Newman's novels are still reprinted and read. Besides their historical and biographical value, they contain many humorous, eloquent, and satirical passages.

Newman spent the remainder of 1847 in Rome and in visiting Oratorian establishments and shrines in various cities of Italy. Several conferences with the Pope were used to determine his future work in England, for which Newman set sail on December 6.

CHAPTER 3

Founder and Lecturer

NEWMAN arrived in London from Rome on December 23, and he returned to Maryvale on January 1, 1848. His associates subsequently arrived there, and the English Oratory was formally inaugurated on February 2. Since it was located in the diocese of Birmingham, it became more popularly known as the Birmingham Oratory. Newman served as superior of the community, as novice master for its aspirants, and as lecturer in theology. At forty-seven, he complained of loss of vigor in meeting the challenging tasks of leading a new venture; he frequently felt the weight of his responsibility and would have preferred to be much younger.[1]

Preaching became one of the main activities of the English Oratorians. Father Wilfrid Faber, with Newman's consent, inaugurated a project of familiarizing English Catholics with some biographies of modern Saints. But too many objections arose; and, on the ground that they did not suit the tastes of English readers, Bishop William P. Ullathorne, who had succeeded Wiseman as bishop of Birmingham, suggested withdrawal of the project. Newman acquiesced to Ullathorne's wishes, but only after much hesitation.[2]

The increase of new members, as well as some disagreements pertaining to religious exercises and the zeal of the younger members for efforts to make conversions, led to the founding of other Oratorian houses.[3] In October, 1848, a temporary arrangement was made at St. Wilfrid's, Cheadle, until a permanent Oratory was opened on Alcester Street, Birmingham, on February 2, 1849. Newman also took advantage of Bishop Wiseman's suggestion to establish an Oratory in London, where Wiseman had been transferred. The London Oratory was formally opened on May 31, 1849.

While in Birmingham, Newman frequently preached **to**

crowded congregations composed of Protestants as well as Catholics. When the sermons were published as *Discourses to Mixed Congregations* in November, 1849, some readers regarded the sermons as stern; others viewed this sternness as a result of spiritual insight, desirous of arousing those smugly complacent about religious matters to be aware of the illusive attraction of sin and temptation.[4] The style of these sermons is considered more ornate—similar to the French pulpit orators, Bossuet, Bourdaloue, Massillon—than the sermons preached at St. Mary's, Oxford.[5] The sermons portray the enthusiasm of a convert, who, no longer wrestling with doubt, possesses "a mature self-confidence and a vigor of style which bring out all the more vividly his special powers as a preacher. His sermons now have a new character; they are passionate, boldly imaginative, colorful, at times consciously rhetorical." [6]

I Difficulties of Anglicans

On March 8, 1850, the British Privy Council issued a decision overruling an Anglican bishop's refusal to install G. C. Gorham as a vicar of a parish because he had denied the doctrine of baptismal regeneration. Anglicans stubbornly objected at this interference of the civil power over the spiritual, especially since the bishop had upheld an orthodox Anglican belief. When Newman was called upon for public comment, he preferred at first to let "the Gorham case" speak for itself. Friends, however, were able to convince him, and Newman reluctantly decided to give a series of lectures which have been published as the first volume of *Lectures on Certain Difficulties Felt by Anglicans*. The lectures began on May 9, 1850, and continued for twelve weeks. Since they were delivered in the London Oratory, they have also been called the "King William Street Lectures" after the address of the Oratory. While preparing the lectures, Newman expressed his reluctance: "I am writing them intellectually against the grain more than I ever recollect doing anything." [7]

In the first seven lectures, Newman argues that the true outcome of the Oxford Movement of 1833 should be communion with Rome. He directs his arguments specifically to the Tractarians who had followed him but who had remained in the Anglican Church because they were hesitant about joining the Church of Rome. He challenges the very *raison d'être* of Anglicanism:

"We see in the English Church, I will not merely say no descent from the first ages, and no relationship to the Church in other lands, but we see no body politic of any kind; we see nothing more or less than an Establishment, a department of Government, or a function or operation of the State—without a substance,—a mere collection of officials, depending on and living in the supreme civil power." [8] Thus, he hit at the crux of the problem in the Gorham case.

To those who felt that the Oxford Movement was merely an effort to reform the Anglican Church, Newman poses these questions: "Is the Establishment's life merely national life, or is it something more? Is it Catholic life as well? Is it a supernatural life? Is it congenial with, does it proceed from, does it belong to, the principles of Apostles, Martyrs, Evangelists, and Doctors, the principles which the movement of 1833 thought to impose or to graft upon it, or does it revolt from them?" [9]

With all the logic at his command, Newman substantiates his arguments that the Oxford Movement had been "foreign to the National Church," that it had not derived any strength from it, and that it had originated and developed independent of it. Rather the movement had a providential course—not in the direction of the National Church, nor to any party or sect in it, and certainly not to seek or form a Branch Church—but clearly to lead to the one and only true apostolic Church of Rome.

The last five lectures aim at resolving the difficulties of Anglicans in accepting communion with Rome as the one, holy, catholic, and apostolic church. Aware of the popular criticism of the socio-economic status of many European Catholic countries in the nineteenth century, Newman insisted on a clarification of the mission of the church. The church does not aim for the worship of material goods and comfort or for the establishment of a worldly paradise:

The Church aims not at making a show, but at doing a work. She regards this world, and all that is in it, as a mere shadow, as dust and ashes, compared with the value of one single soul. She holds that, unless she can, in her own way, do good to souls, it is no use her doing anything; she holds that it were better for the sun and moon to drop from heaven, for the earth to fail, and for the many millions who are upon it to die of starvation in extremest agony so far as temporal affliction goes, than that one soul, I will not say should be lost, but should commit one single venial sin, should tell one wilful untruth, though it harmed no one, or steal one poor farthing without excuse. She considers the action of the world and the action of the soul as simply incommensurable, viewed in their respective spheres.[10]

In the Roman Catholic Church's sacramental system Newman observes a source of warmth and spiritual strength in contrast to the coldness of Protestant worship.[11] Where the Church of England finds it difficult to command agreement in matters of faith on even fundamental tenets, the Church of Rome, composed of diverse nationalities—so diverse that she can claim universality—possesses unity of faith on all basic doctrine while she admits free discussion about undefined matters and maintains authority to censure heretical and schismatic tendencies.[12] Newman's concluding lecture, "Ecclesiastical History No Prejudice to the Apostolicity of the Church," reaffirms the necessity of tracing apostolic succession from the present to the first apostles.

When these lectures led to a number of conversions, including clergymen, Anglican rebuttal of the lectures consisted largely in attacking the motives of Newman and the converts rather than in replying to the arguments. Such was the technique employed especially by Sir Frederick Rogers in a series published in the *Guardian*. A Newman critic, however, has acknowledged the brilliance of his lectures: "His exposition of the weakness of the Anglican position is devastating, and yet it arouses no unnecessary antagonism. There is no unfairness, no cheap sarcasm, no empty rhetoric." [13] Richard H. Hutton, an Anglican who attended the lectures, but who continued his disagreement with their arguments and conclusions, wrote, "Never did a voice seem better adapted to persuade without irritating"; and he felt that the published lectures were Newman's first book to be read generally by Protestants.[14]

II   The Present Position of Catholics in England

In July, 1850, Bishop Wiseman was called to Rome. Some of the older priests in London—with whom he was unpopular because of spending money accumulated by his predecessors for building Catholic institutions and because of his boasting about the progress of Catholicism in England in a manner that caused resentment among non-Catholics—had hoped for Wiseman's transfer. But, while in Rome, it was announced that Wiseman had been elevated to Cardinal Archbishop of Westminster with all the English Roman Catholics under his jurisdiction. Although Wiseman did not return to England until November 11, he sent to English Catholics on October 7, a week after his appointment, a pastoral letter entitled, "From out of the Flaminian Gate of Rome." In it he declared that "the great work then is complete. . . . Your beloved country has received a place among the fair Churches which, normally constituted, form the splendid aggregate of Catholic Communion: Catholic England has been restored to its orbit in the ecclesiastical firmament, from which its light had long vanished, and begins now anew its course of regularly adjusted action round the center of unity, the source of jurisdiction, of light, and of vigor." [15]

When Cardinal Wiseman's letter was read to all of his congregations, it could have appeared to them as a signal triumph for Roman Catholicism in England; but, when the pastoral letter appeared in English newspapers, without interpretation and explanation, a storm of protest arose. Suggestive of a Roman conquest in England, Wiseman's letter appeared as a willful act of aggression against national independence. Cries of "No Popery" and "Down with tyranny" were heard, and the Pope and Wiseman were burned in effigy throughout England. Informed of the furor his letter had incited, Wiseman, even before returning to London, began the writing of another letter, "Appeal to the English People." When the English newspapers printed the letter in full, on November 20, both the words and the tone of this second letter assuaged the fears of "aggression" which the first letter had created.[16]

Newman, however, realized that despite the favorable reaction to Wiseman's second letter, a cloud of suspicion still hung over Roman Catholics in England. He, therefore, felt that an analysis of the reasons for this suspicion would help create a more favorable climate of opinion. Roman Catholicism was misunderstood, he was convinced, because it had been misrepresented for many years. Consequently, he began preparation of a series of nine lectures under the title of *The Present Position of Catholics in England*. These lectures, delivered in the Corn Exchange in Birmingham in the summer of 1851, were published in book form later the same year.

The purpose of *Present Position* is twofold: (1) "with a view of suggesting to them, how best, as Catholics, to master their own position and to perform their duties in a Protestant country"; and (2) not "to prove the divine origin of Catholicism, but to remove some of the moral and intellectual impediments which prevent Protestants from acknowledging it." [17]

Newman's literary technique in this volume is most unlike any of his other works. Sarcasm, scathing satire, caricature, and irony are employed; little self-restraint is shown by one whose personality was by nature shy and self-composed. His humor brought laughter that could be heard outside the building.[18] But such was Newman's intent; he wanted to bring to a *reductio ad absurdum* the many false impressions held by non-Catholics. He emphasized repeatedly that the Protestant view of Roman Catholicism stemmed from ignorance—a fact which to him required patient understanding and logical explanations: "Having once been a Protestant, and being now a Catholic—knowing what is said and thought of Catholics, on the one hand, and, on the other, knowing what they really *are*—I deliberately assert that . . . the absurdities which are firmly believed of Catholics by sensible, kind-hearted, well-intentioned Protestants . . . [are] the consequence of having looked at things all one side, and shutting the eyes to the other." [19]

In four of the lectures, Newman demonstrates how fable, logical inconsistency, prejudice, and assumed principles are responsible for Protestant misconceptions. Granted a wrong twist of logic and of historical facts, Protestants have nevertheless incorporated these misconceptions into an "immemorial" and "unauthenticated" tradition, passed on from person to person, from generation to generation, in the manner in which tales are told.[20] Tradition, therefore, has been the sustaining power of the Protestant view. But, since Newman was not a one-sided thinker, he also acknowledged that some misconceptions were based on true testimony. To deny, for example, the existence of scandals would be to imply that the Catholic Church contains within her pale but the just and holy—an ideal never promised by Christ to His Church. To employ an effective argument against the Catholic Church, Protestants "must show, not that individuals are immoral or profane, but that the Church teaches, or enjoins, or recommends, what is immoral or profane; rewards, encour-

ages, or at least does not warn and discountenance, the sinner;
or promulgates rules, and enforces practices, which directly lead
to sin." [21] In his concluding lecture, Newman admonishes his coreligionists, especially the laity, to lead lives that exemplify what
their religion stands for in their daily contact with the society
in which they live. Newman regarded these lectures as the best
written of all his works.[22] They were viewed at the time, and
they are viewed today, as a valuable aid to a *rapprochement* between Catholics and Protestants in England and in the United
States.[23]

Although the lectures may have served to improve relations
between Roman Catholics and Protestants, statements which
Newman made in the fifth lecture concerning an ex-priest, Gia-
cinto Achilli, caused Newman personal embarrassment. When
Achilli had arrived in England from Italy in 1850 after having
been deposed from his priestly office, he had begun a campaign
of slanderous attacks on Catholic Church teachings and clergy,
and he had found receptive audiences in England because of
Wiseman's pastoral letter establishing the hierarchy. Aware of
Achilli's background and of the credence that could be given to
his statements as a former Catholic priest, Newman decided to
expose him by using information considered reliable, which had
been printed in the *Dublin Review*. Therefore, he used Achilli as
"an incontrovertible proof that priests may fall and friars break
their vows" and proceeded to catalog his offenses.[24]

Achilli not only denied the charges but sued Newman for libel.
The trial did not begin until June 21, 1852. Despite the evidence
amassed by Newman's attorneys and the testimony of witnesses,
the jury found Newman guilty. The London *Times* strongly condemned the verdict and attributed it to anti-Catholic bigotry.[25]
Application for a new trial was denied; and on January 31, 1853,
the judge pronounced a fine of one hundred pounds and impris-
onment until the fine was paid, which it was on that very day.
The Achilli trial drew indignation from both Catholics and non-
Catholics. The English people had seen through Achilli; and they
became convinced that Newman had suffered a grave injustice.
Achilli lost all his support, left England, and went into oblivion;
and Newman could write, "Sympathy is doing for me here, what
success would not have done." [26]

While Newman was still immersed in the details of the Achilli trial, he preached on July 13, 1852, one of his most brilliant sermons, "The Second Spring." The occasion was the First Provincial Synod of the Roman Catholic bishops of England held at St. Mary's, Oscott; and Cardinal Wiseman presided at this commemoration of the establishment of the new hierarchy. In his sermon, documented by historical facts and motivated by his desire to promote understanding and acceptance of his faith in the country he loved, Newman developed the theme that "the English Church was, and the English Church was not, and the English Church is once again." [27] Newman delineates the glorious role of Roman Catholicism in the past, especially mentioning the English who were canonized as saints; he unoffensively depicts Roman Catholicism's death in England at the hands of the authorities of the Crown; and he announces that "the winter is now past, . . . the flowers have appeared in our land . . . [and] fulfill to us the promise of this Spring." [28]

In probably the first recorded appreciation of this sermon, Bishop Ullathorne, writing during the synod, noted that "Dr. Newman preached one of his best sermons, and had the bishops, and divines—most of them—weeping, for half an hour." [29] Newman, enthusiastically greeted afterwards, could not himself escape the display of strong feelings which the sermon produced.[30] Considered a "moment of Romantic triumph," a characteristic evaluation of "The Second Spring" is: "Firm, sensitive and thrilling with an emotion which runs along all its harmonies, the composition is a poem, to be judged by its correspondence with a scene in history which could not be acted over again." [31]

III *The Catholic University of Ireland*

Newman was not only to be the founder of the Oratorians in England and a lecturer on theological topics; he was also to occupy a similar role in education. On July 8, 1851, Archbishop Paul Cullen of Armagh, Ireland, arrived in England to ask Newman to be the founding rector of the Catholic University of Ireland. Newman's acceptance of the post became the occasion of *The Idea of a University,* a series of lectures giving his rationale for a college education—his best-known work and one regarded as a classic in the field of education by both Catholics and non-Catholics.

The need for a Catholic university in Ireland had its roots in history.[32] From 1600 to 1793, the period of penal laws against Catholics, no Catholic could attend a university or go to the Continent to do so. With the passage of the Catholic Relief Act of 1793, Catholics were permitted to attend universities and also to establish their own schools; but few Catholics had ever had the means to avail themselves of a university education.[33] On July 31, 1845, a significant event in Irish educational history occurred when a bill to establish three colleges in Ireland became law. They were to be called Queen's Colleges and were to be supported by the state and be non-sectarian. A meeting of the Irish bishops was held to examine this government educational project, and a majority of the bishops expressed the opinion that the colleges would be dangerous to the faith and morals of Roman Catholics. Instead of considering the purpose of the colleges according to the intent of the law—"the extension of improved education to all classes in Ireland"—the bishops branded them as "Godless" and as "a deliberately devised instrument to subvert the Catholic faith." [34] The bishops, therefore, formally opposed their attendance by Catholics. When the bishops who did not concur with this decision appealed to Rome, the Pope supported the majority view; and the Irish bishops subsequently issued a pastoral letter on September 9, 1850, affirming their prohibitive stand.

Although the Irish bishops initiated plans in January, 1849, for establishing a Catholic university for Irish students, it was not until a year later that a committee, of which Archbishop Cullen became the chairman, was selected to make concrete plans. In an *Address to the People of Ireland,* the committee formally announced its intention and enunciated the overall aim of its educational endeavor: "The Catholic Church . . . looks upon the work of education as only half done unless diligent moral culture and practical piety proceed *pari passu* with intellectual improvement." [35]

However, no unanimity of support for a university came from Irish Catholics. The graduates of Trinity College, Dublin, saw no need for it; in loyalty to their alma mater, they felt that Catholics could receive a higher education at Trinity, even though it was an institution under Anglican sponsorship. Many of the clergy thought that Catholics did not have the financial means to maintain a Catholic university. Catholics opposed to the idea of higher education regarded the venture as unnecessary. One element that favored the university regarded it as an ecclesiastical seminary for the training of the clergy, and Archbishop Cullen belonged to this faction.

Against this background, Newman arrived in Dublin to deliver his lectures between May 10 and June 7, 1852. Aware of the lack of agreement among the Irish as to the necessity and the nature of a university under Catholic sponsorship, Newman decided that two main topics should be emphasized. The need and role of theology in education required thorough explanation—aimed at the Trinity graduates and at those unwilling to make a sacrifice for a religion-orientated education. The true nature of a liberal education and its value in developing the mind were to be delineated—aimed at Catholics opposed to higher education and at the faction favoring a seminary, which did not distinguish between a university education and professional training.

Newman, moreover, also realized that he had some personal problems in lecturing to the Irish. In his introductory discourse, therefore, he sought to render himself acceptable by dwelling on those objections that his listeners might see in him personally. He was an Oxford graduate, and the Irish were trying to establish a non-Oxford university. But he demonstrated that his Oxford experiences have acquainted him with university education and its main problems, especially as to the role of religion and the nature of a liberal education. He was a convert from Protestantism; he, therefore, had the advantage of viewing education in the natural order, whereas Catholics seem to stress the supernatural order. Furthermore, he intended to present a view of education that should be acceptable to all religions. Newman was a foreigner and an Englishman; but, in speaking to the Irish, he did so with the authority of the Pope, who "knows no distinction of races in his ecumenical work." [36] Besides, in the matter of education, the English and the Irish have had a long tradition "in the interchange of kind offices and the rivalry of love." [37]

Newman first deals with the role of theology in education. He points out that, since a university teaches all knowledge and since theology is a branch of knowledge, a university should teach it. If the study of theology is eliminated, then theology would be regarded not as knowledge but as opinion. Theology, like other branches of knowledge, is a scientific study. It is not to be equated with Catholicism or acquaintance with the Scriptures; nor does it consist of pious or polemical remarks about the physical world. Theology is the science of God—of God in Himself and of God in relation to the world and to the beings He has created. By compromising on the study of theology, "you will soon break up into fragments the whole circle of secular knowledge." [38]

Moreover, theology should be studied not only because it is itself a science but also because it has relevance to other branches of knowledge. The division of knowledge is an artificial barrier for the purpose of clarity and efficiency; for "all that exists, as contemplated by the human mind, forms one large system or complex fact, and this of course resolves itself into an indefinite number of particular facts, which, as being portions of a whole, have countless relations of every kind, one towards another." [39] The systematic omission of any branch of knowledge prejudices the accuracy and completeness of knowledge, and human knowledge has interrelatedness only because it has a unifying force: Truth is One, and God is Truth. In studying creation in its manifold manifestations, man studies the Creator:

All knowledge forms one whole, because its subject-matter is one; for the universe in its length and breadth is so intimately knit together, that we cannot separate off portion from portion, and operation from operation, except by a mental abstraction; and then again, as to its Creator, though He, of course, in His own Being is infinitely separate from it, and Theology has its departments towards which human knowledge has no relations, yet He has so implicated Himself with it, and taken it into His very bosom, by His presence in it, His providence over it, His impressions upon it, and His influences through it, that we cannot truly or fully contemplate it without in some aspects contemplating Him. [40]

The elimination of any science from the circle of knowledge encourages the other sciences to use the vacancy created and thus to usurp functions not their own. The omission of theology would involve not only the loss of one science but the perversion of the other sciences. Whenever theology is dropped, its place of preeminence will be usurped by other sciences entirely unsuited for that position: "Religious Truth is not only a portion, but a condition of general knowledge." [41]

Newman begins his discussion of the nature of a liberal education in a discourse entitled, "Knowledge Its Own End." By knowledge Newman means not information but mental culture or excellence, or what he termed "a philosophical habit of mind" with the qualities of freedom, equitableness, calmness, moderation, and wisdom. He who possesses such a mind "apprehends the great outlines of knowledge, the principles on which it rests, the scale of its parts, its lights and its shades, its great points and its little, as he otherwise cannot apprehend them." [42] This philosophical habit of mind is the result of a liberal education—the purpose of a university. Using the words of Aristotle, Newman defines a liberal education: *"liberal, which tends to enjoyment, . . . where nothing accrues of consequence beyond the using."* [43] As a humanist philosopher of education, Newman views knowledge as its own end; for liberal education perfects man's intellect and is justified for that reason alone.

The advantages of a liberal education are seen in contrast to an education whose sole object is utility or professional skill. Newman does not deny the value and need of professional training; instead, he emphasizes that it must be preceded by a liberal education. Training merely in a specialized branch of knowledge leads to a stinted, stunted mind, one which is lost outside its own field and cannot comprehend the broad horizons of human knowledge. Without a liberal education, "it is the common failing of human nature, to be engrossed with petty views and interests, to underrate the importance of all in which we are concerned, and to carry out partial notions into cases where they are inapplicable, to act, in short, as so many unconnected units, displacing and repelling one another." [44] A man may have superior skill in his department, but "he is in danger of being absorbed and narrowed by his pursuit." [45] "His virtues, his science, and his ideas are all to be put into a gown or uniform, and the whole man to be shaped, pressed, and stiffened, in the exact mould of his technical character." [46]

The liberally trained mind, for Newman, is prepared not solely for one professional skill but for all skills; for man's judgment is employed in all skills. And judgment is "that master-principle of business, literature and talent, which gives him strength in any subject he chooses to grapple with, and enables him to seize the strong point in it." [47] Liberal studies train man's power to judge; they give exercise to the judgment. History furnishes fullness;

moral philosophy, strength; poetry, elevation to the understanding. Liberal studies, moreover, not only aid one another but also serve as a check upon each other. History presents things as they exist, disfigured and perverted by human passion; philosophy strips the picture too much; poetry adorns it too much; but "The concentrated lights of the three correct the false peculiar colouring of each, and show us the truth." [48] The liberally trained mind, therefore, has the power to analyze and synthesize; it has undergone an "enlargement."

The passage best known and most often quoted of all of Newman's writings is his description of a gentleman—"one who never inflicts pain." [49] The gentleman, with his cultivated intellect, is characterized by patience, understanding, prudence, resignation, kindness, consideration, forbearance, empathy, gentility, tolerance, candor, broad-mindedness, courtesy, delicacy of taste, refinement, equitableness, modesty. [50] Too frequently these characteristics are set forth as Newman's idea of a gentleman, but readers of Newman are mistaken if he regards the possession of these qualities as the highest attainment, for in addition to having the attributes of a gentleman (which are desirable as far as they go) one must strive for supernatural perfection, which is not within the scope of a liberal education. A liberal education, even under pagan auspices, can produce the qualities of a gentleman. Newman's view of the gentleman is one refined not only by knowledge but also by supernatural grace. The Christian must turn to St. Paul for the picture of a Christian gentleman, patterned according to principles of evangelical perfection. It is he who "draws the Christian character in its most graceful form, and its most beautiful hues." [51] Newman referred to St. Paul's chapter on charity in the first Epistle to the Corinthians, which Fulton Oursler has termed "the most glorious words ever written by man" in "the greatest letter ever written." [52]

With all its advantages, a liberal education for Newman cannot produce, however, supernatural perfection: "Knowledge is one thing, virtue is another; good sense is not conscience, refinement is not humility, nor is largeness and justness of view faith. . . . Liberal Education makes not the Christian, not the Catholic, but the gentleman." [53] As a humanist, Newman emphasized the role of a liberal education in advancing intellectual excellence. But, as a Christian humanist, he understood the weakness

of human nature and, *a fortiori*, the limitations of a liberal education without the orientation of theology as a subject of study
and without religion as an inspiring force in man's intellectual
and spiritual development. He almost borders on Calvinism in
distrusting human nature: "Quarry the granite rock with razors,
or moor the vessel with a thread of silk; then may you hope with
such keen and delicate instruments as human knowledge and
human reason to contend against those giants, the passion and
the pride of man." [54]

The final lecture, "Duties of the Church towards Knowledge,"
reiterates the role of theology in education, which can be achieved
properly only when the church has jurisdiction over a university.
Newman chooses physical science and literature as the areas of
learning for which the interposition of the church is necessary.
An unnecessary hostility has arisen between religon and physical
science; their object of study is the same—God's world. But their
methods differ: theology is deductive; physical science, inductive.
Since "a sinless Literature of sinful man" cannot be had, young
minds require the church's guidance in interpreting the literature
of history.[55]

Having delivered the last of his Dublin lectures in June, 1852,
Newman returned to England. The Achilli libel case, which had
been caused by Newman's remarks in the fifth lecture of *The
Present Position of Catholics in England* in the summer of 1851,
was now ready for court trial and, as already discussed, held
Newman's attention until January, 1853. Furthermore, sickness
and personal dissensions among the members of the various
oratories required his personal attention. He had to attend to
these matters before fully embarking on the university venture.
But the university was uppermost in his mind; and the selection
of a faculty became a prime concern. He had little success in
recruiting his old Oxford friends, who probably would not have
received the endorsement of Archbishop Cullen. The archbishop
preferred to make his own appointments both to the faculty and
administrative posts. Newman wrote to Cullen in July, 1852, that
he would be quite agreeable to the choice of any professor as
long as he possessed the necessary qualifications; but he insisted
emphatically that the vice-rector should be his own personal
appointment. Cullen, however, proceeded with his own appointee.
Nor did Cullen honor Newman's request for the creation of a

committee to assist him as rector in planning the establishment
of the university and for his formal installation as rector. Need-
less to say, Newman began to have serious misgivings as to his
possible success in Dublin.[56]

In January, 1853, Newman wrote to Cullen for a formal commission from the Irish bishops to inaugurate the university. But
Cullen replied neither to this letter nor to subsequent letters of
February and of March. Not until January 4, 1854, did Cullen
send Newman the formal request to come to Ireland. Meanwhile,
Newman had written to Cardinal Wiseman concerning the delay;
and Wiseman, having already heard of Newman's difficulties,
had mentioned the situation to Pope Pius IX and had suggested
to the Pope the necessity of promoting Newman to the office of
bishop so that he would have not only a rank equal to the Irish
bishops but also additional prestige for the office of rector.[57]
Cullen, however, exerted his own influence in Rome; and he
urged no such rank for Newman on the grounds that it would
cause an unnecessary expense to support the rector as a bishop,
that the Irish people would resent an Englishman as a bishop in
their midst, and that, furthermore, not even the rector of the
famed University of Louvain in Belgium enjoyed such a distinction.[58] As a result, Newman never received the expected honor;
nor was he ever given an explanation for its not being conferred.[59]

When Newman arrived in Dublin on February 7, 1854, he
found that varied opinions still existed as to the purpose of the
university—his lectures on university education apparently had
influenced very few—and he set out to visit personally the Irish
bishops in the hope of gaining support. Sickness prevented his
discussing the subject with all of them, but he did feel some
progress was made with the few he had contacted. He was
formally installed as rector in June, and he made plans for the
opening of the university in the fall.

On November 9, the School of Philosophy and Letters was
opened. Newman chose as the topic for his inaugural address,
"Christianity and Letters." In an eloquent plea he emphasized
the role of the Classics in the training of the mind and in the
background essential for a truly educated person: "The literature
of Greece, continued into, and enriched by, the literature of
Rome, together with the studies which it involves, has been the
instrument of education, and the food of civilization, from the

first times of the world down to this day." [60] The Classics, further-more, may be called "the soil out of which Christianity grew." [61] But Christianity, Newman continued, perfected the heritage of mankind, as it is the complement and fulfillment of the religious heritage of Jerusalem. In Rome converged the two great fountain-heads of sacred and profane learning to give the world today the Judeo-Christian, Greco-Roman heritage—the foundation of West-ern Civilization.

With the university formally inaugurated, Newman could at-tend to the many details required for its daily functioning. His ability as an educational administrator became evident with the formulation of a handbook to guide the university's operation. McGrath, in his comprehensive study of Newman in Dublin, re-gards the *Rules and Regulations* as "the most detailed and definitive document available to illustrate the actual working of the University, and is a proof of Newman's broad grasp of general aims, combined with a severely practical attention to detail." [62] Uppermost in Newman's mind as projects he wished to initiate during his tenure in office were a university church, as a center of religious and intellectual influence on the campus; the publica-tion of the *Catholic University Gazette,* as a medium for the exchange of ideas among professors and for the acquaintance of the public with the function of the university; the establishment of a medical school, to which would be added later a chemical laboratory and an astronomical observatory; and the fostering of the study of Celtic literature. He succeeded in establishing all four projects. However, Newman had no success in obtaining a charter from the British government for the university to grant academic degrees, and he objected to any compromise plan which would have permitted his students to obtain their degrees from one of the Queen's Colleges, feeling that such an arrangement weakened the very purpose of a Catholic university. [63]

Newman's fame as a university educator rests not upon his being an administrator but upon his being an expositor of univer-sity education. [64] The lectures he delivered and the essays he wrote in Ireland are still read and quoted today; they have be-come classics in educational literature. Many of these lectures and essays were published in 1856 in a volume entitled *The Office and Work of the Universities* (more commonly known today as *University Sketches* and included in most editions of *The Idea of a University*); others are contained in Volume III of *Historical Sketches* published in 1872. Newman dealt with basic issues involved in a university education, inquiring, for example, "What Is a University?" And he offered as its *raison d'être* the ancient concept of a university as a *Studium Generale,* or "School of Universal Learning." The modern devotees of educational specialization would find in Newman's description of a university their most formidable challenge:

A University is a place of concourse, whither students come from every quarter for every kind of knowledge. . . . It is the place to which a thousand schools make contributions; in which the intellect may safely range and speculate, sure to find its equal in some antagonist activity, and its judge in the tribunal of truth. It is a place where inquiry is pushed forward, and discoveries verified and perfected, and rashness rendered innocuous, and error exposed, by the collision of mind with mind, and knowledge with knowledge. It is the place where the professor becomes eloquent, and is a missionary and a preacher, displaying his science in its most complete and most winning form, pouring it forth with the zeal of enthusiasm, and lighting up his own love of it in the breasts of his hearers. It is the place where the catechist makes good his ground as he goes, treading in the truth day by day into the ready memory, and wedging and tightening it into the expanding reason. It is a place which wins the admiration of the young by its celebrity, kindles the affections of the middle-aged by its beauty, and rivets the fidelity of the old by its associations. It is a seat of wisdom, a light of the world, a minister of the faith, an Alma Mater of the rising generation.[65]

Loyal to his concept of a university, Newman was a staunch advocate of free discussion of all ideas; for he insisted that "great minds need elbow-room, not indeed in the domain of faith, but of thought. And so indeed do lesser minds, and all minds." [66] All subjects of human thought should be open for consideration: "Nothing is too vast, nothing too subtle, nothing too distant, nothing too minute, nothing too discursive, nothing too exact, to engage its attention." [67] With a policy of "Live and let live," he would encourage professors of the different branches of knowledge to pursue truth according to the methods peculiar to their fields, collecting data and formulating principles, arriving at conclusions that may conflict with the research of professors in other departments, yet noting what conclusions concur, where and why they disagree, distinguishing between real and apparent difficulties, and avoiding positions evidently untenable due to lack of pertinent data or insoluble by human reason.[68]

In encouraging reason to have its fair and full play, Newman would submit to the Hegelian dialectic of proceeding from thesis to antithesis until a satisfactory synthesis is achieved. That errors would naturally result, Newman conceded; but the human mind's path to truth is circuitous; there are no short cuts, no straight avenues, and no guarantee that the mind can be prevented from getting lost along the way. To prevent liberty of investigation is to deny the very possibility of investigation.[69] Newman would adhere to the Italian dictum *sbagliando impariamo* ("we learn by making mistakes"); and he, therefore, could calmly assert that "Error may flourish for a time, but Truth will prevail in the end. The only effect of error ultimately is to promote Truth." [70]

Nor did Newman exclude either free discussion in matters religious or the possibility of conflict between secular knowledge and theology. "That is no intellectual triumph of any truth of Religion, which has not been preceded by a full statement of what can be said against it." [71] Presupposing that there is loyalty to revealed truth and a deep sense of responsibility, the scholar is free to pursue research even where there is an apparent contradiction or confusion with teachings of the church. But the scholar is admonished not to become "the nervous creature who startles at every sudden sound, and is fluttered by every strange or novel appearance which meets his eyes." [72] He must stay within the bounds of his own discipline and commit his problem to sober reflection and "to Time, the great interpreter of so many secrets." [73] If Galileo had restricted his doctrine of the motion of the earth as a scientific conclusion and left the interpretation of Scripture to those whose province it belongs, Newman felt that much unnecessary controversy would not have arisen.[74] When this lecture is viewed in the light of the *Essay on Development*, modern religious thought can well profit from the many investigations in physical science, psychology, and Scriptural linguistics that theology requires for devising a faith to meet the needs of the present-day and not some remote, antiquated past.

With all the freedom of discussion that he desired in academic

life, Newman, however, always insisted on the preeminent role
of theology. In the essay, "A Form of Infidelity of the Day," he
condemned the sentiments of those who sought to regard religion
as merely opinion and not as a scientific study; for the result
would be that if theology is not considered knowledge, then its
study must be considered a waste of time, and the teachers of
theology enemies of the progress of human thought.[75] He also
opposed the policy of removing theology from its role of preeminence in the curriculum. The tactic of these nineteenth-
century infidels was twofold: negatively, that they should not
argue about theology or even seek to exclude it from schools, for
such action would only focus attention upon it and incite the
proponents of theology to plead its cause; positively, that they
should rival theology by preoccupying students' minds with other
subjects, especially with physical science, by working on the
imagination to make students think that religion is false because
it disagrees with what they are already familiar, and by so presenting the results of science that its tangible facts and practical
results appear as the guarantors of human progress.[76] The rise of
secularist humanism in education testifies to Newman's accurate
analysis of the policy of infidelity.

Newman, the liberal educator *par excellence*, discussed in
essays and lectures the value and role of other academic disci-
plines in the curriculum. He defined grammar as the scientific
analysis of language whereby the meaning of words are known
separately and in relation to other words in a sentence. Translating English into Latin requires a knowledge of the different
grammatical constructions peculiar to each language, and he
recommended parsing words as evidence of accurate understanding.[77] In a satirical fashion, he contrasts two students in their
entrance examinations to college by depicting their training in
accuracy of expression. How applicable for today is his observa-
tion on those who "shrink from the effort and labours of thinking and the process of true intellectual gymnastics":

The consequence will be that, when they grow up, they may, if it so
happen, be agreeable in conversation, that they may be well informed
in this or that department of knowledge, they may be what is called
literary; but they will have no consistency, steadiness, or perseverance;

they will not be able to make a telling speech, or to write a good letter, or to fling in debate a smart antagonist, unless so far as, now and then, mother-wit supplies a sudden capacity, which cannot be ordinarily counted on. They cannot state an argument or a question, or take a clear survey of a whole transaction, or give sensible and appropriate advice under difficulties, or do any of those things which inspire confidence and gain influence, which raise a man in life, and make him useful to his religion or his country.[78]

In the lecture "Literature," delivered to the School of Philosophy and Letters, Newman examined the nature of this academic area and offers criteria for evaluating literary works. Newman regarded literature as essentially a personal work, "the personal use or exercise of language," by which the writer expresses his own ideas and feelings.[79] Where science would be primarily concerned with things and objective truth, literature portrays thoughts and subjective truth. The peculiarities of individuals give language its character. Literature projects the writer's personality: his ideas, thoughts, feelings, imaginations, aspirations, abstractions, comparisons, discriminations, judgments upon life, views of external things, wit and humor, sagacity—"the very pulsation and throbbing of his intellect."[80] Accurate and clear reflection of thought must characterize a writer's style, for "style is a thinking out into language."[81] Newman would, therefore, reject any goal as *ars gratia artis.* The dealer in words writes simply for effect and cares little for the subject he embellishes; his literary labors consist in artistic fastidiousness, elaborateness, ornamentation, collocation of words.[82]

In "English Catholic Literature," Newman enlarged on the integrating role of theology set forth in his *Idea of a University.* "Catholic" pertains not merely to religious topics or to writings by ecclesiastics. An English Catholic literature would include all subjects of knowledge treated as a Catholic would treat them, in view of the bearing of theology on all knowledge. When a literature is formed, it becomes a rational and historical fact. A Catholic university in an English-speaking country must add to that nation's heritage. "Every great prophet has a character of its own, which it manifests and perpetuates in a variety of ways."[83] The following passage suggests the role that the study of literature, Catholic or non-Catholic, has in the curriculum:

The growth of a nation is like that of an individual; its tone of voice and subjects for speech vary with its age. Each age has its own propriety and charm; as a boy's beauty is not a man's and the sweetness of a treble differs from the richness of a bass, so it is with a whole people. The same period does not produce its most popular poet, its most effective orator, and its most philosophic historian. Language changes with the progress of thought and the events of history, and style changes with it; and while in successive generations it passes through a series of separate excellences, the respective deficiencies of all are supplied alternately by each.[84]

Although, as rector of the Catholic University of Dublin, Newman was contributing to educational literature by his lectures and essays and was engaged in a work he deemed of great value to the people and culture of Ireland, he continued to have misgivings about the future of his university and to be beset by other problems. A charter was never granted; conflict about the practical goals of the university continued with Archbishop Cullen and other Irish prelates—leading Newman to question the success of the university; and the appointment of Englishmen as professors was resented by the Irish. Trips to England became more and more necessary as misunderstandings in regard to the work of the Oratorians arose among other religious orders and among the Oratorians themselves.[85] Newman also complained of physical fatigue, arising especially from his journeys between Dublin and London.[86] As a result of these difficulties, Newman, after only two years of guiding the university, gave serious consideration to resigning from the rectorship; but not until April, 1857, did he write his official letter of resignation, designating November 14 as the effective date.[87]

To Newman's surprise, many of the Irish bishops insisted on a reconsideration or at least a postponement of his withdrawing from the university; and even Archbishop Cullen joined in an effort of establishing some compromise to induce Newman to remain.[88] It was suggested to Newman that he could continue as rector while spending more time in England, with a vice-rector entrusted with the daily management of university affairs. Newman accepted the compromise proposal, but it was never fulfilled, as no agreement could be reached about the choice of a vice-rector acceptable to both Newman and Cullen.[89] Newman, therefore, decided to make his resignation final; and exactly seven years after his acceptance of the Dublin post, on November 12, 1858, he announced his complete severance from the university. Technically, he remained as rector until the official acceptance by the Irish bishops on August 10, 1859. The Catholic University of Ireland in Dublin continued as organized by Newman until 1879, when it became a constituent college of the Royal University of Ireland and was partially endowed by the British government. In 1908 it became a constituent college of the National University of Ireland.[90]

Newman's university has survived as an idea rather than as a reality. Circumstances and personalities converged to militate against the realization of the idea that he had forcefully outlined in his lectures on university education. Even biographers sympathetic to Newman have not hesitated to hold him culpable. "He had not the driving force necessary to make a success of a struggling institution," concluded Bertram Newman;[91] and he had "hardly an organising head," believed Canon Barry.[92] But the personalities who cultivated many of the unfavorable circumstances for the university offer a strong testimony about Newman's ability. In requesting reconsideration of his resignation, the Irish bishops wrote in 1857 that because of "the able and zealous manner in which he has discharged the duties of Rector of our Catholic University, we are as anxious now to perpetuate those services to our rising University, as we were at first to secure them." [93] Upon Newman's appointment as a cardinal in 1879, his successors at the university offered him this encomium: "The plan for higher education and the system of University government which you initiated and organized, will, centuries hence, be studied by all who may have to legislate for Catholic education, as among the most precious of the documents which they shall possess to inform and guide them." [94] In his authoritative study of Newman's university work, McGrath concluded that "Newman left in Ireland a living exemplar of the noble idea which he had sketched in immortal prose, the idea of a university courageously treading every field of human knowledge." [95]

But it was Archbishop Cullen, once Newman's chief adversary, who rose above differences of opinion and personality to laud Newman. When some of Newman's writings were being questioned for their orthodoxy at Rome, Cullen emerged not as the devil's advocate but as Newman's boldest champion; and, in a pastoral letter to his people, he referred to Newman as one "whom Ireland will ever revere." [96]

IV Callista

During the summer of 1855, while on vacation in England from the university, Newman completed *Callista: a Sketch of the Third Century,* his second and final novel. This work was begun in 1848, but "Sheer inability to devise personages or incidents" led to his putting the work aside for seven years.[97] Two writings appear to have occasioned *Callista.* Charles Kingsley had published in 1853 the historical novel, *Hypatia,* a sympathetic exposition of pagan life and thought during the fifth century. Its treatment of monasticism, the value of celibacy, and the alleged infringement of Christianity upon philosophical thought offended Roman Catholics. Cardinal Wiseman's *Fabiola,* a novel about the early Christian martyrs during the Roman persecutions, was published in 1854; and its popularity reminded Newman of his own unfinished novel and served as a stimulus for completing it.[98]

Callista is "an attempt to imagine and express the feelings and mutual relations of Christians and heathens" in the third century.[99] The heroine, Callista, is a beautiful pagan girl living in the small town of Sicca near Carthage in North Africa, a part of the Roman Empire in the reign of the persecuting emperor Decius. With her brother, Callista sculptures and paints pagan statues and idols. She falls in love with a convert to Christianity, Agellius, who desires to marry her and also to convert her. Agellius' uncle, Jucundus, agrees to the marriage in the hope that Callista will be able to reconvert him to paganism; but the opposite begins to occur as Callista shows signs of interest in Christianity. However, before either the marriage or the conversion of Callista to Christianity can take place, a plague of locusts ravages the territory. Enraged by the devastation of their farms, the pagan populace seeks an explanation and holds culpable the rulers of Sicca whose policy of leniency towards the Christians failed to implement the imperial decrees restricting their activities; thus the gods were offended.

An infuriated mob, which takes the law into its own hands, goes in search of Christians, including Agellius, who cannot be found; but Callista, not yet Christianized, is captured and imprisoned. Her long, quiet hours in a prison cell afford her the opportunity of reading St. Luke's Gospel, which had been given to her by Caecilius, the exiled bishop of Carthage and a friend of Agellius. Her first acquaintance with the Christian Scriptures leaves her undecided; and, when interrogated by the civil authorities, she denies being a Christian but refuses to pay reverence to the pagan Roman gods. Her brother, Aristo, engages the services of Polemo, a popular pagan philosopher of Carthage, to try to convince her of Christianity's fallacious reasoning and to return her to paganism. Polemo, however, fails in his mission; for Callista, upon rereading St. Luke's Gospel, becomes convinced of Christianity and unequivocally abjures the religion of her birth. Caecilius, informed of her request for conversion, secretly manages to baptize her in prison. When news of her conversion becomes known, she is put on trial and condemned to death on the rack. Agellius succeeds in recovering her body, Caecilius conducts her burial service, and Callista works miracles after her death. Agellius is raised to the episcopacy, and is also martyred for his faith.

As in Newman's other novel, *Loss and Gain,* the element of suspense is lacking in *Callista;* the reader can quickly perceive the outcome of the novel from the start. Although the characters are more successfully individualized, they still remain "shadowy outlines" with few physical traits.[100] A critic of his novels felt that "you would never recognize any of Newman's characters if you met them in the street."[101] Notwithstanding these defects, *Callista* does portray the interplay of minds and emotions between Christians and pagans in the third century. Roman life and manners are skillfully represented; and today's Christian becomes more appreciative of his freedom to worship. Enjoyable is Newman's description of the plague of locusts as the reader notes a flash of literary brilliance.

They smear every thing they touch with a miserable slime, which has the effect of a virus corroding, or, as some say, in scorching and burning it. . . . And like snow did they descend, a living carpet, or rather pall, . . . Heavily and thickly did the locusts fall, . . . they choked the flame and the water . . . and the vast living hostile ornament still moved on. . . . They dim the bright marbles of the walls and the gilding of the ceilings. . . . They move along the floor in so strange an order that they seem to be a tasselated pavement themselves. . . . Wherever man has aught to eat or drink, there they are, reckless of death, strong of appetite, certain of conquest.[102]

CHAPTER 4

Years of Frustrating Endeavors

I *Translation of the Bible*

NEWMAN, while still serving as rector of the Catholic University of Ireland, was informed in 1855 by Bishop Ullathorne that it was decided at a meeting of the English bishops to entrust to him the supervision of a new English translation of the Bible. But not until August 26, 1857, did Cardinal Wiseman send the official notification to him. Having profited from his experiences with the Irish bishops, Newman requested to see the actual decree before accepting; Wiseman obliged; and Newman formally accepted the task on September 14, stating that "a greater honour could not possibly have been done" him.[1] Wasting no time in making the necessary preparations, Newman began to search for the most competent Scripture scholars. The need for a new English edition of the Bible was readily apparent: the standard version for English-speaking Catholics was the sixteenth-century Douay-Rheims Bible, revised in the middle of the eighteenth-century by Bishop Richard Challoner. A more modern translation was desired.

For more than a year Newman and his collaborators attended to their task. Meanwhile, Newman and Wiseman engaged in correspondence as to who should hold the copyright. Newman requested holding it temporarily until the Holy See gave the project final approbation. Wiseman rejected his request but did not offer any financial aid for the expenses being incurred. Since Newman was forced to meet the expenses with his own resources, he was eventually permitted to have the copyright for himself.[2] The reason for the hesitancy of the English bishops for clarifying their stand on the copyright became evident when Newman received from Wiseman a letter written by the American bishops, which questioned the value of Newman's project because Archbishop Francis P. Kenrick of Baltimore had already commenced a new English version of the Scriptures, part of which had even been published.

Attached to the letter was a resolution of the American bishops deprecating the need of two independent projects and suggesting to the English bishops one English version in which Newman and Kenrick could collaborate. Newman expressed his willingness to participate in a cooperative venture if the English bishops granted their approval, and he requested his translators not to proceed any farther in their work, subject to a possible change of plans. The English bishops, however, gave no indication of their intentions. After waiting two years for a reply, Archbishop Kenrick wrote to Newman of his proceeding with the American version without hope of collaboration from English Catholics. Newman replied to Kenrick in July, 1860, stating that he had been "in some suspense as to the intention of the English prelates with respect to it" and charitably assigned Wiseman's busy schedule and illness as "the cause of the silence which I am sorry you should have felt to be an inconvenience." In this gentlemanly manner Newman congratulated Kenrick on the progress already made and expressed hope for successful completion.[3]

Without formal word from Wiseman, it became clear to Newman that work on the Bible translation should cease. Whether it was because of the influence of booksellers with large stocks of the Bible on hand, who might have pressured Wiseman, or jealousy on the part of other English ecclesiastics who might have coveted the honor of a new version, or just plain indifference on the part of the English hierarchy, the English Catholics were left without a modern Catholic version of the Bible for nearly another century.[4] Furthermore, what estimate can be made of the loss to the English-speaking world of God's inspired word rendered in Newman's brilliancy of style?

II *The Periodical* Atlantis

While involved with the Bible translation project, Newman became concerned with the manner in which English Catholics were meeting objections against their faith. Evolution had rocked many traditional religious views, and devout Christians found themselves intellectually inadequate to cope with the many questions that arose as to the relation between science and religion, the Bible's account of the creation of man and the world, and the theories of evolution. Newman felt that a genuine contribution could be made by inaugurating a magazine whose special purpose would be to analyze the relations between religious faith and human reason. Thus originated in 1858 the periodical *Atlantis,* of which Dr. W. K. Sullivan, a professor of medicine at the Catholic University of Dublin, became the editor and Newman the chief mentor.[5] The goal of *Atlantis* was not to be controversial but to provide a means for both clergymen and laity to be kept abreast of the trends in scientific research and to consider their possible bearing on religion. The extremes of stubborn conservatism and rash speculation in relation to scientific theories were considered destructive to sound theology—a new type of *via media* for Newman.

But hardly had *Atlantis* been launched than the appointed ecclesiastical censor took objections to a proposed article which sought some reconciliation between a too-literal interpretation of the Bible and the tendency of modern rationalists to change or modify religious doctrines on the basis of scientific findings and such theories as evolution. Newman, fearing unfavorable reaction, recommended that the article not be published: "I have found lately that some good friends of mine are taking great liberties (at least in their thoughts) with me, and are looking at everything I do in the way of theology, and I feel certain I shall be whispered about at Rome if it appears. At my time of life, with so many things to do and so many interests to protect, I have no wish for a new controversy and quarrel in addition to the many in which I am engaged." [6]

Newman, however, was convinced of the need for establishing an acceptable *rapprochement* between faith and reason; and he sought to prepare a more favorable climate with one of his own articles, "The Benedictine Centuries," in the January, 1859, issue of *Atlantis.*[7] To substantiate the logic of his approach Newman appealed to the history of thought in the Christian Church. He contrasted the conservative role of the Benedictine schools in the eighth and ninth centuries with the creative thought of the thirteenth century. When man lived in periods of deep religious faith, conservatism was acceptable. The Scriptures were read and accepted; the exegesis of the Fathers of the Church went unchallenged. And Newman portrayed the Benedictine monk in his seclusion from the world, undisturbed by novel speculations, as follows:

The monk proposed to himself no great or systematic work, beyond that of saving his soul. What he did more than this was the accident of the hour, spontaneous acts of piety, the sparks of mercy or beneficence, struck off in the heat, as it were, of his solemn religious toil, and done and over almost as soon as they began to be. If to-day he cut down a tree, or relieved the famishing, or visited the sick, or taught the ignorant, or transcribed a page of Scripture, this was a good in itself, though nothing was added to it tomorrow. He cared little for knowledge, even theological, or for success, even though it was religious. It is the character of such a man to be contented, resigned, patient, and incurious; to create or originate nothing; to live by tradition. He does not analyze, he marvels; his intellect attempts no comprehension of this multiform world, but on the contrary, it is hemmed in, and shut up within it. It recognizes but one cause in nature and in human affairs, and that is the First and Supreme; and why things happen day by day in this way, and not in that, it refers immediately to His will.[8]

The Greco-Arabian philosophical movement, however, shattered the complacency of Western medieval civilization. The Arabians Avicenna (980–1037) and Averroës (1126–1198) interpreted the philosophy of Aristotle in such a manner that the medieval mind was confronted with a view of the world that contradicted religious faith. The teaching of Aristotle was interpreted so as to destroy traditional concepts of God and the world. It was imperative for Christian philosophers and theologians to meet the challenge: "theology required to be something more than the rehearsal of what her champions had achieved and her sages had established in ages passed away. . . . Hardheaded objectors were not to be subdued by the reverence for antiquity."[9] St. Thomas Aquinas in the thirteenth century became the bold champion of faith and revelation by a novel approach. He studied Aristotle's works and synthesized Aristotelian philosophy with Christian theology. Where Avicenna and Averroës had made Aristotle the enemy of faith, Aquinas' new philosophy, Scholasticism, made him an ally. To have remained conservative in the thirteenth century would have caused disaster to Christian thought; the dynamic, creative mind of Aquinas securely defended it.

Theology could not confront the doubts and confusion, the new challenges in the nineteenth century brought about by science by means of old theological principles. Creativity of thought, for Newman, would be urgently needed to "discriminate, rescue, and adjust the truth which a fierce controversy threatens to tear in pieces, at a time when the ecclesiastical atmosphere is thick with the dust of the conflict, when all parties are more or less in the wrong, and the public mind has become so bewildered as not to be able to say what it does and what it does not hold, or even what it held before the strife of ideas began." [10] The contribution of such an endeavor as *Atlantis* would consist of meeting the challenge of modern rationalism and of aiding the desired *rapprochement* between faith and reason. "To restore the multitude of men to themselves and to each other by a reassertion of what is old with a luminousness of explanation which is new, is a gift inferior only to that of revelation itself." [11] Doctrine not only had its own development, but it required new approaches to meet new challenges.

Atlantis was a publication of the Irish university, and with Newman's withdrawal from the rectorship his direction of the periodical also ceased. Issued twice a year, it continued until 1870 in fulfilling its original purpose of explaining new scientific discoveries and their relation to religious teaching; but many literary contributions were also included. Its influence on contemporary thought was questionable, as Newman was reminded in 1861 when he submitted an article for publication: "The story goes that you have sent to the *Atlantis* a paper on the classics . . . , but the *Atlantis* never appears and the world has forgotten it." [12]

III *The* Rambler *Affair*

Shortly after the first issue of *Atlantis* in 1858, another periodical engaged more of Newman's attention—the *Rambler*. An Oxford friend, later a convert, John Moore Capes, founded a Catholic review in 1848 and became its editor; but laymen were its contributors. Although Newman declined the invitation to be its ecclesiastical censor, he nevertheless maintained an interest in the periodical and was frequently consulted about proposed articles.[13] He encouraged the laymen's aim of stimulating the thought of educated Catholics by acquainting them with the latest intellectual and scientific developments and with the consequent effect on religious doctrine. He felt that the laymen's more intimate contact with the non-Catholic mind could produce more practical exposition of religious dogma than the cloistered cleric's strict adherence to the proofs of the theology textbooks.

From the start, the writers of the *Rambler,* however, were too prone to rash speculation about scientific matters and too extravagant in their statements about doctrinal matters. They antagonized many readers with their sharp criticism of traditional Catholic apologetics as being ineffective in meeting the challenge of modern agnosticism. Although they perceived the problems caused by nineteenth-century trends on religious faith, the laymen lacked adequate philosophical and theological training to prevent them from reckless writing.

Newman had been aware of Capes's difficulties for many years, but in 1857 he became "pained" and "almost frightened" at the tone of the articles. "Capes is too good a fellow," he noted, "for one to have any fears of *him,* but his articles both register, and will blow up and spread, bad feeling,—very bad feeling." [14] Still sympathetic to the *Rambler's* overall aim, Newman considered his forthcoming return to England as "providential" because of the possibility that he might be in a position to direct the efforts of the periodical: "The Bishops are necessarily engaged in the great and momentous ecclesiastical routine. They are approving themselves good stewards . . . while the party of the aristocracy and the party of talent are left to themselves without leaders and without guides." [15]

Several times in 1858 when Newman corresponded with Capes, he indicated erroneous interpretations and applications of theological reasoning.[16] Capes subsequently resigned the editorship and was succeeded by Richard Simpson, his sub-editor, also a convert. Sir John Acton became part owner of the publication and Simpson's closest collaborator. Influenced by liberal German Catholicism and by its leading exponent, the theologian and historian Ignatius Döllinger, Simpson and Acton launched the *Rambler* into a policy of extreme liberalism. They argued for scientific freedom and a reconsideration of religious doctrine in the light of new scientific theories. Although they acknowledged ecclesiastical authority, they were quick to deride the failings of the men who held it; and they documented their statements with churchmen's scandals, which English Catholics had never heard of or had believed to be Protestant fables. In the burning and complex issue of the temporal sovereignty of the papacy, they expounded the extreme liberal position which sought to deny the Pope of any political sovereignty. Cardinal Manning, in the meantime, strongly supported the necessity of this sovereignty.

By 1859 the *Rambler* had thoroughly alienated the English bishops and was regarded as an object of irritation and deep concern. It was even learned that the English bishops were to issue a pastoral letter censuring the periodical. In the hope of preventing an action certain to be explosive, Bishop Ullathorne was commissioned to ask Newman, known for his acquaintance and friendship with the *Rambler*'s editors and writers, to secure Simpson's resignation. Newman thus was caught in a web from which it was almost impossible to become disentangled: he sympathized with the aims of the periodical, but he also knew that the bishops had decided on its death. Simpson hesitated at first to relinquish what he considered an important cause; he even threatened to continue its publication in spite of any action by the bishops. But Newman was able to assuage Simpson and the bishops by means of a plan that promised to avert unfavorable publicity and dissension among his coreligionists: the *Rambler* was to continue; and, at Wiseman's request, Newman was to be its editor. Newman had apparently achieved a diplomatic victory: Simpson was satisfied about the continuance of publication; and the bishops felt safe with Newman in charge.

In March, 1859, Newman assumed the editorship of the *Rambler*. Convinced that such a medium was necessary for an educated laity, he sought to eliminate its previous offensive and vitriolic tone. "To create a body of thought as against the false intellectualism of the age, to surround Catholicism with defences necessary for and demanded by the age, to take a Catholic view of and give a Catholic interpretation to the discoveries of the age"—these would be Newman's goals for the *Rambler*.[17]

Newman never intended to continue as editor of the *Rambler* beyond the fulfillment of his aim of making it a creditable organ of Catholic thought. But, as Trevor has remarked of his new

involvement, it "was rather like asking Newman to carry a box
of explosives through a burning house." [18] Too many viewed the
Rambler with suspicion. And in Newman's first issue—May, 1859
—the fires of suspicion were fueled. In a column commenting on
"Contemporary Events," written but unsigned by him, Newman
stated: "We do unfeignedly believe . . . that their Lordships
[the English bishops] really desire to know the opinion of the
laity on subjects in which the laity are especially concerned. If
even in the preparation of a dogmatic definition the faithful are
consulted, as lately as in the instance of the Immaculate Conception, it is at least as natural to anticipate such an act of kind
feeling and sympathy in great practical questions." [19]

A "practical question" of immediate concern to English Catholics in the 1850's was governmental aid to their schools. In 1858,
Parliament had set up a commission to study the means of extending "sound and cheap elementary instruction to all classes
of people." Catholic laymen, including those associated with the
Rambler, wanted to cooperate openly with public authorities.
Money was not their sole concern, but rather the image of the
Catholic school. If opened to public inspection, the emphasis
on preparing youth for citizenship could be seen and thus bigotry
and suspicion would be lessened, or even completely eliminated.
There would be no compromise with the content of religious
instruction, for only the methods of instruction would come under
public supervision. At the same time, but importantly, Catholic
schools would receive public subsidies.

The Roman Catholic bishops of England had been invited to
participate in discussions with the Royal Commission. Furthermore, the laity had organized in 1847 a Catholic Poor School
Committee to serve as liaison between their bishops and the
government on educational questions. In November, 1858, the
bishops instructed their clergy not to cooperate with representatives of the Royal Commission; for the bishops strongly felt that
the admission of government inspectors into Catholic schools
would lead to the state's exercising authority over religious matters.[20]

S. Nasmyth Stokes of Trinity College, Cambridge—a convert,
the secretary of the Catholic Poor School Committee since its
inception, and a government appointed inspector for schools—
wrote in the *Rambler* issue of January, 1859, an article entitled,

"Royal Commission on Education." In it, he questioned: "What henceforward is to be the attitude of the English Catholics towards the Crown and Parliament of Britain? In the progress of civilization and the advance of popular liberty, shall we, by showing honour and respect to the civil magistrate within his legitimate sphere, prove ourselves fit inhabitants of a land of freedom? or shall we, by adopting the principles of those 'whose infirm and baby minds are gratified by mischief,' strengthen the worst prejudices of our religious and political opponents?" [21]

This situation formed the immediate background of Newman's comment on "contemporary events" in the May, 1859, *Rambler* issue. In full realization of the suspicious attitude of the bishops and of the sincerity of the many laymen, he offered in conciliatory tone an explanation.

If our words or tone were disrespectful, we deeply grieve and apologize for such a fault; but surely we are not disrespectful in thinking, and in having thought, that the Bishops would like to know the sentiments of an influential portion of the laity before they took any step which perhaps they could not recall. Surely it was no disrespect towards them to desire that they should have the laity rallying round them on the great question of education. . . . If we have uttered a word inconsistent with this explanation of our conduct,—if we argued in a hard or disrespectful tone,—if we put into print what might have been better conveyed to their Lordships in some other way,—we repeat, we are deeply sorry for it. We are too fully convinced of the misery of any division between the rulers of the Church and the educated laity.[22]

But, when objections immediately arose to the explanation, Newman accepted responsibility for its publication. Bishop Ullathorne, in agreement with the adverse criticisms of the *Rambler* and under the "general impression that the old spirit was not clean gone out of the periodical," asked Newman for his resignation, effective after the July issue.[23] Although Newman complied in conformity with ecclesiastical obedience, he felt an obligation toward his friends among the laity; and he insisted on returning the periodical to the direction of its owners, Acton and Simpson— an act honorable from the viewpoint of business ethics but dangerous ecclesiastically. He had now more than ever identified himself with the suspect group.

In July, 1859, the explosion came. The *Rambler* published an article by Newman, "On Consulting the Faithful in Matters of Doctrine." Readers viewed the article in the context of the controversial laymen editing the *Rambler* and of the article which had occasioned Newman's resignation. The article went beyond the mere practical level of inquiring from the laity their views and feelings as to matters like education, for Newman raised a major theological issue in referring to the sentence in the May issue: "In the preparation of a dogmatic definition, the faithful are consulted." Two questions, he maintains, must be answered: whether an "appeal" to the faithful ought to be considered as a preliminary to defining a doctrine of faith and whether with this appeal to them they can rightly be considered as "consulted." [24]

Semantics plays a role in the use of the word "consulted." In the Latin language and in theological writing, "consulted" means "to take counsel with, to ask for a judgment." In the English language the meaning also includes the asking for factual data. When the faithful are consulted, then, it is for determining what their belief is as a "matter of fact, . . . as a testimony to that apostolical tradition, on which alone any doctrine whatsoever can be defined." [25] If Newman had stopped at this point in the discussion and had concluded that "consulted" meant merely ascertaining a matter of fact, he could have avoided, perhaps, additional confrontation with those who cast suspicion on his religious orthodoxy. Instead, he argued beyond the "wording" and stated that the Holy See had treated the faithful "with attention and consideration . . . because the body of the faithful is one of the witnesses to the fact of the tradition of revealed doctrine, and because their *consensus* through Christendom is the voice of the Infallible Church." [26] Newman insisted that the laity represented only one of the sources for ascertaining the historical tradition of the Church; others included the bishops, theologians, liturgical rites, ceremonies, and customs, events, disputes, and movements throughout the church's history. [27]

Skillfully, Newman proceeded still farther in his discussion by claiming that, while different theologians may stress one source in preference to another, he would lay great stress on the *consensus* of the faithful because the Church has, when other sources have been obscure or silent, referred to the laity's beliefs and devotional practices. And he documents his statements with the statements of learned theologians and with specific instances in history when the Pope did seek out the sentiments of the people, as was done in 1854 with the proclaiming of the doctrine of the Immaculate Conception.[28]

The essay's *pièce de résistance* comes when Newman praises the loyalty of the faithful in adhering to orthodox views in the fourth century while bishops had become tolerant of the heresy of Arianism. He states: "In that time of immense confusion the divine dogma of our Lord's divinity was proclaimed, enforced, maintained, and (humanly speaking) preserved, far more by the *Ecclesia docta* than by the *Ecclesia docens;* that the body of the episcopate was unfaithful to its commission, while the body of the laity was faithful to its baptism." [29] Newman continues for twenty-five pages of the essay with documentation and evidence to support his thesis "that the Nicene dogma was maintained during the greater part of the fourth century, not by the unswerving firmness of the Holy See, Councils, or Bishops, but by the 'consensus fidelium'." [30]

Bishop Brown of Newport interpreted the article "On Consulting the Faithful" as an example of a convert's rashness and theological ignorance; to him, it appeared that Newman had accused the infallible church of having fallen into error. With other bishops and theologians in agreement as to the article's implication, Brown took the initiative of formally delating the article to Rome. Before even asking or permitting Newman to offer any clarifications, Brown wrote to the authorities in Rome: "It is most painful to see published, by one whom we regarded as one of the best of our converts, allegations and arguments such as have been put forward again and again, by our heretical enemies, which have as often been refuted, and which might have been the writing of a Calvinist." [31] Nor was Brown satisfied; he appealed to Monsignor George Talbot, an Englishman with a position of influence at the Vatican, to bring the heretical stand of Newman to the personal attention of the Pope. Pius IX was reported as having been disappointed in Newman, but he did not take any official action against him. Nevertheless, Newman became suspect among church leaders in Rome and in England; the impression fostered was that he entertained unorthodox views and that his loyalty to the Holy See could not be trusted.

The action of the English bishops in regard to his article on the laity and to the *Rambler* led Newman to frustration. "I did all I could," he wrote to a friend,

to ascertain God's will—and that being the case, I am sure good will come of my taking it—I am of the opinion that the Bishops only see one side of things, and I have a mission, as far as my own internal feelings go, against evils which I see—on the other hand I have always preached that things which are really right, still are done, according to God's will at one time, not another—and that if you attempt at a wrong time what in itself is right, you perhaps become a heretic or schismatic. . . . When I am gone, it will be seen perhaps that persons stopped me from doing a work which I might have done. God rules over all things. Of course it is discouraging to be out of joint with the time, to be snubbed and stopped as soon as I begin to act.[32]

Even more sadly he wrote, as he reminisced, "All my life I have been plucked, . . . I never meant to keep it [the *Rambler*] for long—but it is one thing to set a thing off, another to be made to throw it away." [33] Had he been permitted to continue the *Rambler,* he could have succeeded in moderating the periodical's tone. Instead, after being restored to Simpson, its rash attacks continued on traditional church policy. In 1860 the seminary training of the clergy was characterized as inadequte to meet the needs of the times. The writer, H. N. Oxenham, documented his position with Newman's view of a liberal education as given in his lectures in Ireland. In 1861, at a time when the papal states were being attacked by Sardinian leaders in their plan for the unification of Italy, the periodical questioned the temporal power of the papacy. When authorities in Rome were informed of this desertion to the side of the revolutionary liberals, Manning was directed to place the *Rambler* under ecclesiastical censure. Knowing that such an act would alienate all support, the editors acquiesced in suspending publication—a move with which Newman concurred.[34]

But, even after Newman's withdrawal from the *Rambler,* his name was still associated with the unorthodox periodical. Wiseman and Ullathorne discussed Newman while they were in Rome in 1860. Because of the unfavorable impression which had been formulated about Newman in Rome, Wiseman asked Newman to submit a detailed explanation of his views, demonstrating their possible orthodoxy and loyalty to the Holy See, or even a retraction of them. Newman did send such an explanation to Wiseman, who showed it to Manning and Talbot; but the letter of explanation was not transmitted to the Pope or to any authority in Rome.[35] Newman feared going to Rome to explain his views in person, and in consequence Rome considered him indifferent as to whether he was considered heretical or not. Suspicion hovered over him.[36] Now approaching sixty, Newman felt that old age prevented him from acting aggressively. He acquiesced to failure as God's will for him. His writings were not selling, and his loyalty to his church of adoption was seriously questioned. Despondently, he remarked that those in authority "have put me on the shelf." [37] He willingly withdrew into a self-imposed period of silence.

What was there for Newman to do? He contemplated the revision of previous writings, and he put in order his private papers.[38] He occupied himself with the teaching and spiritual direction of boys at the Birmingham Oratory School, which he had founded after his return from Ireland. But this endeavor, too, vexed him, for its headmaster and several instructors resigned in 1861 because of Newman's alleged favoritism towards individual personnel in the school; thereafter, he depended on Ambrose St. John for the school's active direction.[39] For the most part, however, Newman continued his withdrawal from potential controversies; prayer and tilling his garden became his pastimes.

Wonderment at his silence caused inquiry. He replied to one query in 1862:

Seven reason for not writing more books. I do not write
(1) because in matters of controversy I am a *miles emeritus, rude donatus.*
(2) because no one serves on Parliamentary Committees after he is sixty.
(3) because Rigaud's steam engine which was hard to start was hard to stop.
(4) because Hannibal's elephants never could learn the goose-step.
(5) because Garibaldi's chaplains in ordinary never do write.
(6) because books that do not sell do not pay.
(7) because just now I am teaching little boys nonsense verses.[40]

But Newman's reasons for silence were not readily accepted, even when so facetiously expressed. As his despondency began to be generally known, rumors began circulating that he was contemplating returning to the Anglican Church. Newman denied these rumors in letters to individuals who wrote to him,[41] but he made no public disavowal until the *Lincolnshire Express* reported a speech which had asked, "What has become of the great 'giant' of intellect and sanity—John Henry Newman? I [G. Noel Hoare, the speaker] have the authority of a clergyman of high church caste, . . . for saying he has become utterly *sceptical;* and as for believing . . . in the Creed of Pope Pius IV (that Shibboleth of Romanism concocted in the 16th century) he absolutely ridicules it and the Romish persuasion altogether." [42] Newman publicly replied in the London *Globe* with a categorical denial of any possible rejection of the Roman Catholic Church; and, with seldom-employed sarcasm, he posed the question, "I am tempted to ask in turn, who is this Mr. G. Noel Hoare? In an age of light, where in the world has the unfortunate man been living?" [43]

The years 1859 to 1864 have been termed "the low-water mark of Newman's life story." [44] Frustrating endeavors had marked his career; despondency and even sometimes bitterness had been evident in his correspondence. But he viewed the perennial struggle of good and evil in the perspective of Christian faith: the victory of good was inevitable. Burdened by the sad days of these years, he still entertained hope for the future, as the poem "The Two Worlds," which he wrote in 1862, expresses:

> Unveil, O Lord, and on us shine
> In glory and in grace;
> This gaudy world grows pale before
> The beauty of Thy face.[45]

CHAPTER 5

Victor in Controversy

NEWMAN was not to remain long in self-imposed silence; for, on December 30, 1863, he was mailed anonymously a copy of *Macmillan's Magazine,* in which was a review of volumes seven and eight of Anthony Froude's *History of England.* The sender drew Newman's attention to the following passage in the review: "Truth for its own sake had never been a virtue with the Roman clergy. Father Newman informs us that it need not be, and on the whole ought not to be;—that cunning is the weapon which Heaven has given to the Saints wherewith to withstand the brute male force of the wicked world which marries and is given in marriage. Whether his notion be doctrinally correct or not, it is, at least, historically so." [1]

The review was initialed "C.K."; and Newman sought to ascertain from the publisher the writer of this slandering reference to him. Informed of Newman's request, the reviewer identified himself in a letter to Newman as none other than the Reverend Charles Kingsley, Regius Professor of Modern History at the University of Cambridge, Chaplain to the Queen, a highly popular novelist, an admirer of Darwin, and a dynamic speaker. Kingsley wrote to Newman:

That my words were just, I believed from many passages from your writings; but the document to which I expressly refer was one of your sermons on 'Subjects of the Day,' No. XX, in the volume published in 1844, and entitled 'Wisdom and Innocence.'

It was in consequence of that sermon that I finally shook off the strong influence which your writings exerted on me, and for much of which I still owe a deep debt of gratitude.

I am most happy to hear from you that I mistook (as I understand from your letter) your meaning; and I shall be most happy, on your showing me that I have wronged you, to retract my accusation as publicly as I have made it. [2]

Newman replied to Kingsley's letter by asserting that the sermon to which he referred was preached in 1843 while he was still an Anglican and, furthermore, that he had never uttered the words of which Kingsley accused him or anything that could be interpreted as similar or equivalent to them.[3] Confronted with the dilemma either of offering incontrovertible proof of his accusation or of publicly admitting his error, Kingsley offered instead a statement in the February issue of *Macmillan's Magazine* that could be interpreted as an apology; at the same time, it did not clearly retract his accusation: "Dr. Newman has, by letter, expressed in the strongest terms, his denial of the meaning which I have put upon words. No man knows the use of words better than Dr. Newman; no man, therefore, has a better right to define what he does, or does not, mean by them. It only remains, therefore, for me to express my hearty regret at having so seriously mistaken him, and my hearty pleasure at finding him on the side of truth, in this, or any other matter." [4]

To Newman, this statement was not a forthright retraction of a slanderous remark. Being under suspicion by both Catholics and Protestants, he refused to drop the matter; he desired complete vindication. The experience of previous controversies had taught him that silent retreat only heightens suspicion and creates rumors; therefore, only one path lay before him: to vindicate his own integrity and that of the entire Roman Catholic priesthood, which Kingsley had also slandered. He therefore published in February, 1864, all the correspondence between Kingsley and himself in a pamphlet entitled, *Mr. Kingsley and Dr. Newman: a Correspondence on the Question Whether Dr. Newman Teaches That Truth Is No Virtue?* The pamphlet concluded with a witty caricature of Kingsley's arguments.

But Newman's wit and irony infuriated Kingsley, who deemed it necessary to rejoin in March, 1864, with a pamphlet entitled, *What, Then, Does Dr. Newman Mean?* Kingley's ill-tempered purpose was evident in a note to a friend: "I am answering Newman now, and though of course I give up the charge of conscious dishonesty, I trust to make him and his admirers sorry that they did not leave me alone. I have a score of more than twenty years to pay, and this is an instalment of it." [5] After rehashing the traditional Protestant prejudices against Roman Catholicism, Kingsley accused Newman of approving distortions and exaggerations in a series on the lives of the English saints which he had begun to edit in 1843, but from which he had disassociated himself after only the first two works were published; Newman had explicitly denied responsibility for the contents of these lives.[6] Kingsley portrayed Newman as a fatuous Mariolater, as a cunning equivocator, and as one who assigns precedence to the church over the authority of Sacred Scripture.

I *Writing of the* Apologia

The clarion call had now been sounded for Newman. Kingsley's attack provided him with the opportunity of presenting to the English public a vindication of his whole life—his motives, thoughts, ideals—a genuine *Apologia pro Vita Sua.* Public opinion was sympathetic to him and was disapproving of Kingsley's slanderous approach. Rather than write a book, the completion of which would require months, Newman decided to reply by weekly installments in pamphlet form. On April 21, 1864, the first weekly reply, "Mr. Kingsley's Method of Disputation," was issued. He summarized Kingsley's method as one which would render suspicious anything Newman ever wrote or said; therefore, he would not occupy himself with Kingsley personally but solely with his charges.

In the second issue, "True Mode of Meeting Kingsley," Newman delineated the technique he had adopted to answer the charges. Rather than answer each charge specifically, he offered his readers a development of his religious views, presenting clearly and simply their change and continuity. The readers could thereby judge in proper perspective for themselves the logic and sincerity of his former and present views.

With the third issue commences the opening chapter of the edition of the *Apologia* as subsequently printed in book form; and other issues followed weekly until June 2. At the advice of his friend, Sir Frederick Rogers, Newman eliminated the first two installments from the final edition of the *Apologia* because they might convey an impression of personal sensitivity, sarcasm, and strictures upon the minds of readers.[7] As a result, the *Apologia* is presented as a spiritual autobiography rather than as a work of retaliation; and the name of Charles Kingsley is conspicuous because of its absence.

Although the *Apologia* was written within the short period

of ten weeks, the work is nevertheless the result of endurance and of careful attention to the minutest of detail. Moreover, it was not from memory alone that Newman wrote, for he had meticulously kept his correspondence, and many of his friends also had preserved his letters to them. He checked facts even with those who were still Anglicans and sent them proofs for corrections.[8] Written at the age of sixty-three, the *Apologia* was truly a grueling task for Newman: he wrote from morning to night, hardly having time to take meals; he noted working for as many as sixteen hours a day, and once for twenty-two hours. He admitted to tiring from physical and emotional strain and of finding himself "with his head in his hands crying like a child over the, to him, well-nigh impossibly painful task of public confession." [9]

Four chapters of the *Apologia* describe Newman's religious opinions to the time of his conversion to Roman Catholicism in 1845. Having recorded recollections of thoughts on religious subjects as an adolescent, he was able to offer the impressions that readings and events made on his mind from an early age. It was not until the age of fifteen, however, that he began to form religious convictions.[10] The influences of his educational years, but most especially of his teachers, are set forth. The trends and events that led to his role in the Oxford Movement are reconstructed. His gradual conversion from Anglicanism to Roman Catholicism, with its reasons and even hesitancies, is delineated with candor and logic. The last chapter describes the position of his mind since his conversion—the impact of his newly acquired faith on both mind and heart.[11]

Newman achieved his purpose of vindicating himself in the *Apologia*. Both as a series of pamphlets and as a book, it quickly brought him out of self-imposed obscurity and to national attention. He convinced coreligionists of his sincerity and Protestants of the possibility of accepting Roman Catholicism on the basis of freely exercised logic. As Harrold has observed:[12] "His fame had a 'second spring' almost unparalleled in the annals of authorship." The *Saturday Review* claimed that Newman "has produced one of the most interesting works of the present literary age. Dr. Newman is one of the finest masters of language, his logical powers are almost unequalled, and, in one way or other, he has influenced the course of English religious thought more perhaps than any of his contemporaries." [13] Anglican Bishop E. A. Knox, while in disagreement with the contents, acknowledged that the *Apologia* would "rank for all time among the greatest of the world's autobiographies." [14] An evaluation one hundred years after the publication of the work cites it as "a testament with a special meaning for all Christians in these ecumenical days." [15]

As for what brought about the ready acceptance of and insured continued acclaim for this nineteenth-century autobiography, Harrold's analysis supplies the best answer:

The *Apologia* holds its place among the greatest autobiographies by virtue of its stylistic charm, its remarkable absence of pose (not common to religious or other autobiographies), its simple dignity as it reveals the intimate self of a very sensitive and reserved man. As the narrative proceeds, its style and method vary with the subject and the mood. Whether in plain narration, or in close reasoning, or in portrayal of mental states, the style is ever under complete control and yields absolutely to the demands made upon it. It is by turns persuasive, scornful, pathetic, pleading, conversational, and always deceptively simple.[16]

Newman and his literary masterpiece, however, have not gone unscathed. There were critics, even Roman Catholic ones, who classified the *Apologia* as a classic of "egotism," [17] as "horribly unchristian," as "sickening to read," [18] as "neither a biography nor an autobiography, but simply what it proposes to be, a dialectical apology for a life by the man who lived it," [19] and as "the work of one of the most self-centered men . . . written in a passion of self-admiration." [20] In defense of Newman, however, it must be maintained that *he*—his mind, his feelings, his anguish, his crises—was the subject—but not to the exclusion of all who had shared and contributed to the development of this flux of events and thought. Sensitive by nature, he was capable of empathy in a spirit of "charity towards all, malice towards none." On learning of Kingsley's death in 1875, he promised to pray for him and professed never to have felt resentment toward him, as it was he, "in the good Providence of God, by whom I had an opportunity given me, which otherwise I should not have had, of vindicating my character and conduct." [21] Truly, Newman's unfolding of the spiritual drama of his life can be classified as a spiritual aeneid *par excellence*.

Even Monsignor Talbot, Newman's "devil's advocate" in Rome,

professed to be impressed by the *Apologia*. He subsequently invited Newman to deliver a series of sermons in the Eternal City, an offer to which the Pope gave approval, he wrote. Newman declined, saying that he preferred to continue his work in England and that he had neither the taste nor the talent for the proposal.[22] Newman had not forgotten Talbot's efforts to discredit him with charges of unorthodoxy; furthermore, he viewed with suspicion the sincerity of the invitation and felt that the Pope had had nothing to do with it.[23]

II   The Dream of Gerontius

While engaged in the Kingsley controversy, Newman had a presentiment of impending death. The writing of the *Apologia* in the short period of ten weeks had exhausted him, and a medical opinion had given him cause for concern. The news that Keble had suffered a stroke contributed to this feeling.[24] After the completion of the *Apologia* and after receiving Rome's unfavorable decision on the Oxford plan in early January, 1865, he began to jot down "on small bits of paper" a poetic dramatization of a Christian's death, with which his mind had been preoccupied.[25] This became *The Dream of Gerontius*, written within three weeks. At first, Newman merely put the poem aside; but he submitted it to Henry Coleridge, editor of the Jesuit periodical, *The Month*, when asked for a contribution. *Gerontius* appeared in the issues of May and June, 1865. It was republished separately in November, dedicated to a fellow Oratorian, John Joseph Gordon, who had died in 1853. Gordon was among the first to associate himself with Newman as an Oratorian, and was one of the first of his confreres to die.[26]

The poem begins with Gerontius on his deathbed. Beset by a "strange innermost abandonment, . . . an emptying out of each constituent and natural force," he feels himself sinking "into that shapeless, scopeless, blank abyss, that utter nothingness." [27] Inspired by friends chanting the litany of the dying, Gerontius prays for courage to meet his God and succumbs gradually. Gerontius now finds himself "refreshed" from sleep, not certain whether he is alive or dead; but he is aware of an angel who is holding him "fast within his ample palm," [28] leading him near the judgment court. Nor does Gerontius become frightened by the "sullen howls" of demons, whose blasphemies Newman puts into irregular and harsh rhythms and that Gerontius describes as "how sour and how uncouth a dissonance!" [29] Gerontius then hears angelic choirs singing gracefully in contrast to the demons; he is now in the House of Judgment, where the knowledge of having sinned will be a greater pain than ever before: "The shame of self at thought of seeing Him,—/Will be thy veriest, sharpest purgatory." [30]

As Gerontius comes into "the veiled presence of our God," [31] he again hears the prayers of the friends around his bed. "Consumed, yet quickened by the glance of God," the soul of Gerontius begs for purification:

> Take me away and in the lowest deep
> There let me be,
> And there in hope the lone night-watcher keep,
> Told out for me.[32]

He is committed to the Angels of Purgatory as "a precious soul, until the day, when, from all bond and forfeiture released," he can be reclaimed "for the courts of light." [33] The poem ends with Gerontius' Guardian Angel's bidding his soul "farewell, but not forever," and his requesting bravery and patience; for the "night of trial" shall swiftly pass and he will be awakened "on the morrow." [34]

Throughout the poem are reflected Newman's religious beliefs and his years of thought and experience. He appropriately employed the Roman Catholic Church's teachings on death—spiritual ministration to the dying by the priest, prayers for intercession, the struggle of the soul with evil powers, private judgment of the soul, Purgatory—and with psychological skill indicated their consoling value. His own feelings are apparent; by introspection he offers prognosis of his soul after death, a concern of immediate import when he wrote the poem and characteristic of a personality basically introverted and self-conscious.[35] There was, moreover, a popularity for the poetry of death in Victorian literature, as P. J. Bailey's "Festus," Alfred, Lord Tennyson's *In Memoriam*, Emily Brontë's "Last Lives," Christina Rossetti's "Passing Away," Robert Browning's "Prospice" and "The Guardian Angel," Matthew Arnold's *Memorial Verses*.

Newman's *Gerontius* won immediate acceptance.[36] Encouraged,

Newman collected his poems into a single volume, *Verses on Various Occasions,* and published it in 1868.[37] A French translation of *Gerontius* appeared in 1869; and a German one in 1885.[38] Sir Edward Elgar set it to music in 1900 and portions have become favorite hymns, as "Praise to the Holiest" and "Jesu! by That Shuddering Dread." *Gerontius* has been praised as Newman's "poetic achievement, the fruit of many years of thought and experience." [39]

III   *Oxford Again*

Newman never lost his love for Oxford, and it was no secret that leaving it on the occasion of his conversion caused him much distress. He cherished the learning it had given him and the friends and acquaintances he had made there; he hoped some day to return.[40] In *Loss and Gain* he spoke such sentiments through the main character of the novel. Having gained respect from Catholics and non-Catholics by his successful vindication in the *Apologia,* he realized an opportunity that presented itself in August, 1864. Ambrose Smith, an owner of land near Oxford, offered to sell it to Newman, who immediately recognized its value as a site for an oratory or a hall. Although earlier in the year the English bishops had drafted a resolution discouraging Catholics from attending Oxford, many influential Catholics favored a Catholic college or hall to be established to care for Catholic students at the university. The conviction prevailed that Catholic students should receive the best in education and that the church had not succeeded in achieving this goal in England at this time. When Newman wrote *The Idea of a University,* he brought out the ineffectiveness of an Oxford education for Catholics; but, lacking the ideal Catholic educational set-up, he had seen in this scheme the best alternative.

Bishop Ullathorne approved Newman's plan to establish an oratory near the Oxford campus, but not his plan for a hall, as he was only too aware of his fellow bishops' hostile reactions to such an idea.[41] Newman, therefore, proceeded with the solicitation of funds; but opposition, under the leadership of Henry Edward Manning, an ecclesiastic with influence in England and in Rome, began to arise against him. Cardinal Wiseman was urged to call a meeting of the English bishops, who even decided to submit the idea of an oratory to Rome for an opinion; and

Monsignor Talbot was called upon to use his influence to insure Rome's opposition to any Oxford plan.[42] An attempt by prominent Catholic laymen, many of them converts and Oxford graduates, to present Newman's plan personally at Rome failed; Rome had already been influenced. Early in 1865, Rome sent its official letter of opposition.[43]

Aware that Oxford had no Catholic church, Ullathorne suggested to Newman in March, 1866, that the plan for an oratory be reconsidered. Ullathorne sought Rome's permission; and Cardinal Reisach was empowered by Rome to visit England for the purpose of gathering firsthand information about the Oxford question. Meanwhile, Cardinal Wiseman died, and Manning succeeded him as archbishop. Following ecclesiastical protocol, Reisach conferred with Manning, who carefully selected the "best-informed" for discussion with Rome's representative; but Reisach neither called upon nor consulted Newman about any aspect of the problem.[44] Newman rightfully felt that all hope should be abandoned for the project.[45] However, to his surprise, Ullathorne, notified him on Christmas day, 1866, that Rome had granted permission for an oratory at Oxford and that he could make public the letter formally commissioning him as the inaugurator of the project.[46]

But the following April, after Newman had been making arrangements to reside at Oxford, he received from Ullathorne a letter which forbade his going to Oxford. The letter informed Newman that, with the permission to establish the Oxford oratory, there had been included a "secret instruction" which stated that Ullathorne was to do all in his power to prevent Newman from residing at Oxford.[47] Newman's enemies had been instrumental in achieving this compromise on the Oxford scheme. Newman promised "hearty obedience" to Rome's instruction, but he did feel deeply hurt.[48] As he pondered Rome's decision, he became all the more reconciled. "What is the worth of my voice at Oxford if I am under a cloud," he wrote to his friend James Hope-Scott. As Newman surmised, Rome still had the impression that he maintained unorthodox views; that his editorship of the *Rambler*, especially the essay "On Consulting the Faithful in Matters of Doctrine," had displeased the Pope; and that his attitude and convictions had been constantly misrepresented at Rome by his enemies.[49] Newman subsequently discarded the entire Oxford project; Ullathorne concurred, but accepted the decision "with a sense of pain both acute and deep." [50]

The Oxford project was apparently a failure for Newman in 1867, but time has rendered him the victor in the controversy. For not only Oxford, but practically all non-Catholic colleges and universities throughout the world, have on their campuses Catholic student organizations and even chapels of worship—ones which are appropriately called "Newman Clubs" or "Centers."

IV   Letter to Pusey

In the autumn of 1865, while Newman was in the midst of the Oxford project controversy, Edward B. Pusey published the first of three parts of his *Eirenicon*—an effort toward the reunion of the Anglican Church and the Roman Catholic Church. Ordinarily, Newman would have welcomed any attempt towards reunion or, at least, a better understanding and climate between the two religious communions. Newman and Pusey, moreover, were friends from student days at Oxford and were associates in the Oxford Movement. But Newman felt that Pusey had misrepresented Roman Catholic doctrines, most notably the one concerning the Blessed Virgin Mary. He wrote to Pusey: "It is true, too true, that your book disappointed me. It does seem to me that 'Eirenicon' is a misnomer; and that it is calculated to make most Catholics very angry. And that because they will consider it rhetorical and unfair." [51] Newman acknowledged that some Catholics did hold exaggerated and superstitious views, but he added that "They do not colour our body. They are the opinions of a *set* of people, and not of even them permanently." [52]

Newman, however, was not satisfied merely with a personal reply to Pusey; he chose a public reply in the form of a letter.[53] Entitled *Letter to the Rev. E. B. Pusey on his Recent Eirenicon*, it was the equivalent in length of a book of approximately one hundred and twenty-four pages; but he had written it with the rapidity that had produced the *Apologia* and *Gerontius*. Newman began the *Letter to Pusey* about November 27 and completed it on December 7; it was published the following January. There were two reasons Newman chose a public reply. First, Pusey commanded a position of leadership in the Anglican Church; he was a professor at Oxford, with many followers, known as Puseyites, upon whom he exerted considerable influence. Newman deemed it an obligation to remind Pusey of the possible effect his views could have on others: "There is no one anywhere,—among ourselves, in your own body, or, I suppose, in the Greek Church, who can affect so large a circle of men, so virtuous, so able, so learned, so zealous, as come, more or less, under your influence." [54] Second, Newman, in making a public reply, had the opportunity of demonstrating the extreme position of Roman Catholics, most notably Oxford converts, such as Frederick W. Faber and William G. Ward, on the doctrines concerning the Blessed Virgin Mary and papal infallibility. He could not only answer directly Pusey's charges but also indirectly deal with Faber and Ward in a "most inoffensive way." [55]

Mindful of his friendship with Pusey and of the possible psychological impact of the title as an appeal towards unity, Newman masterfully acknowledges the closeness between the two churches; but he demonstrates the differences between them as well. "There is much both in the matter and in the manner of your Volume, calculated to wound those who love you well, but love truth more. . . . We give you a sharp cut, and you return it. . . . We at least have not professed to be composing an Eirenicon, when we were treating you as foes. There was one of old who wreathed his sword in myrtle; excuse me—you discharge your olive branch as if from a catapult." [56] Newman also qualified Pusey's references pertaining to Anglicanism and Roman Catholicism before his conversion. He insisted on evaluating religious doctrine on the basis of both Scripture and Tradition, especially as contained in the writings of the Fathers of the Church. [57]

Regarding the exposition of the Catholic Church's teaching about the Blessed Virgin, an Anglican writer has concluded that "no simpler, more lucid, or attractive account than Newman's" can be found. [58] Before discussing devotion to her, Newman first examined "the great rudimental teaching of Antiquity from its earliest date concerning her." [59] From a consensus of the Fathers of the Church, he summarized their interpretation of the Bible account of the fall of man and the Blessed Virgin's role in the redemption of man:

She [Eve] co-operated, not as an irresponsible instrument, but intimately and personally in the sin: she brought it about. As the history

stands, she was *sine-qua-non*, a positive, active, cause of it. And she
had her share in its punishment; in the sentence pronounced on her,
she was recognized as a real agent in the temptation and its issue, and
she suffered accordingly. In that awful transaction there were three
parties concerned,—the serpent, the woman, and the man; and at the
time of their sentence, an event was announced for a distant future,
in which the three parties were to meet again, the serpent, the woman,
and the man; but it was to be a second Adam and a second Eve, and
the new Eve was to be the mother of the new Adam. "I will put en-
mity between thee and the woman, and between thy seed and her
seed." The Seed of the woman is the Word Incarnate, and the Woman,
whose seed or son He is, is His mother Mary.[60]

That Mary was the second Eve, who restored what the first Eve
had lost, Newman pointed out, was advocated by St. Justin
Martyr, Tertullian, St. Irenaeus, St. Cyril of Jerusalem, St. Ephrem
of Syria, St. Jerome, St. Peter Chrysologus.[61] From the Church
Fathers, furthermore, certain inferences could be drawn relating
to her sanctity and dignity. Mary's sanctity can best be described
by appropriating to her the title of "Immaculate Conception"—
born without original sin. Newman asked, "If Eve had . . . a
supernatural inward gift given her from the first moment of her
personal existence, is it possible to deny that Mary too had this
gift from the very first moment of her personal existence?" [62]
Newman maintained that misunderstanding of the Catholic
view was largely a problem of semantics. Protestants equate original and actual sin; Catholics see a fundamental distinction. Original sin for Catholics is inherited, a transferal of Adam's sin to
man and, therefore, a negative inheritance. With Protestants
original sin is "a disease, a radical change of nature, an active
poison internally corrupting the soul." According to Roman Catholic thought, as explained by Newman, the angel addressed Mary
as "full of grace" that "for the sake of Him who was to redeem her
and us upon the Cross, to her the debt of original sin was re-
mitted by anticipation." [63]
From Mary's sanctity Newman deduced her dignity. Numerous
titles have been chosen for her, as Mother of life, of mercy, of
salvation; but he asks, "What dignity can be too great to attribute
to her who is as closely bound up, as intimately one, with the
Eternal Word, as a mother is with a son?" [64] Mindful of her role

and dignity, Church Fathers as early as the second century had referred to her as "Theotocos" or "Mother of God." [65]

Newman examined carefully Anglican misconceptions and Catholic excesses in regard to devotion and the intercessory power of the Blessed Virgin Mary. He surrendered such sentiments—such as Mary is infinite, she is superior to God, Christ is subject to her command, Mary alone can obtain a Protestant's conversion, it is safer to seek her than her Son—to Pusey's "animadversion." He acknowledged that he never knew some of these sentiments until he had read Pusey's book, and he doubted that the vast majority of English Catholics ever had heard of them. "They seem to me like a bad dream." [66] Newman also admitted that in the course of time doctrines may be abused (a fundamental point made in his *Development of Christian Doctrine*); nevertheless, he expressed the opinion that "I prefer much wherever it is possible, to be first generous and then just; to grant full liberty of thought, and to call it to account when abused." [67]

By his *Letter,* Newman provided a clear and accurate exposition of the Catholic Church's doctrine about the Blessed Virgin to Pusey; at the same time, he proved that Catholic "extravagances" concerning the doctrine were not founded on Scripture, the Fathers of the Church, or the decrees of Church Councils. He preferred to postpone a discussion of papal infallibility to another occasion; he felt that such a topic was too burning and delicate at the time (Vatican Council I was convoked for considering it in 1869–70). Furthermore, Henry Ryder had written on this subject, which ably showed the untenability of Ward's position. [68]

Newman scored a major victory in his reply to Pusey. The London *Times* treated it as news of national importance and covered it with a long article of seven columns. That Richard W. Church—an eminent Anglican, a leader in the Oxford Movement, and later Dean of St. Paul's Church, London—wrote the article strengthened its impact. "There is only one person on the Roman Catholic side whose reflections English readers in general would care to know," the article said of Newman. It also praised his candor and objectivity by "the English habit of not letting off the blunders and follies of his own side, and of daring to think that a cause is better served by outspoken independence of judgment

than by fulsome, unmitigated puffing." Church reminded Pusey
and his friends to concentrate solely on Ward and Manning,
leaders of extravagant doctrines, who were all the more dangerous because they represented the ruling power in England. "We
want to see some evidence of a public opinion in it [the Roman
Catholic Church] capable of putting them down." [69]

Newman was grateful for the favorable evaluation the press
had rendered him and for the many letters he received in praise.[70]
Ward wrote an article attacking Newman's *Letter to Pusey* and
presented it to Manning for approval. After serious reflection and
consultation with theologians and bishops, Manning urged Ward
not to publish his article—a decision with which even Talbot concurred.[71] Some spurious attacks were issued against Newman for
"coldness towards the Blessed Virgin," but Bishop Ullathorne defended Newman's theology and stated his own personal knowledge of Newman's devotional exercises in Her honor.[72]

Victory in the controversy with Pusey was not accepted haugh-
tily by Newman. He wrote to Pusey that the article in the *Times*
brought him "great satisfaction as being the widest possible ad-
vertisement" of himself.[73] As to Pusey's concern for the harsh
remarks of Ward and his followers about Newman, he added with
gentility, "Thank you for your sympathy about the attacks on me,
but you have enough upon yourself to be able to understand that
they have no tendency to annoy me,—and on the other hand are
a proof that one is doing a work." He expressed sorrow to Pusey
that certain Catholic elements "are so fierce against you. They
have a notion that you are not exact in your facts, and it has put
their backs up; but we are not so exact ourselves as to be able
safely to throw stones." [74] When Newman read in the *Month* issue
of April, 1866, an article he considered unfair to Pusey, he wrote
to the editor: "As to Pusey, I fully think that whatever is misrepresented in facts should be brought out, as well as what is
wrong in theology. . . . Show that Pusey's facts are wrong, but
don't abuse him." And he continued, "to mix up your irrefutable
matter with a personal attack on Pusey, is as if you were to load
your gun carefully, and then as deliberately to administer some
drops of water at the touch-hole." [75]

V Grammar of Assent

The *Grammar of Assent* was published in 1870. Ten years previously, however, Newman had considered a work on "the popular, practical, and personal evidence of Christianity—i.e., as contrasted to the scientific, and its object would be to show that a given individual, high or low, has as much right (has as real rational grounds) to be certain, as a learned theologian who knows the scientific evidence." [76] For not only the *what* of belief but the *how* of belief had preoccupied his mind for many years. With his reading in Bishop Butler's *Analogy of Religion* about 1823 that probability is the guide of life, Newman became profoundly concerned with "the question of the logical cogency of faith." [77] A few years later he wrangled with the concepts of certainty, certitude, the "assemblage" of concurring and converging probabilities.[78]

But Newman realized that it was not only he who desired logical cogency for religious beliefs; in any thinking creature, doubts arise as to the possibility of doctrine not obvious to the senses and not easily explained by reason. He, therefore, frequently preached sermons about the role of faith and reason as, for example, "The Influence of Natural and Revealed Religion Respectively" (1830), "The Usurpation of Reason" (1831), "Faith and Reason, Contrasted as Habits of Mind" (1839), "The Nature of Faith in Relation to Reason" (1839), "Implicit and Explicit Reason" (1840), and "Wisdom, as Contrasted with Faith and with Bigotry" (1841).[79]

In 1838, Newman defined faith as "an original means of knowledge, not resolvable into sense, or the faculty of reason, confirmed indeed by experience, as they are, but founded on a supernaturally implanted instinct developed by religious obedience." [80] But he became all the more aware that, however acceptable such a notion might be to the believer, the agnostic required evidence based on both senses and reason for belief. As he stated in one of his lectures in Ireland:

Christianity has been according to the agnostic the bane of true knowledge, for it has turned the intellect away from what it can know, and occupied it in what it cannot. Differences of opinion crop up and multiply themselves in proportion to the difficulty of deciding them;

and the unfruitfulness of Theology has been, in matter of fact, the very reason, not for seeking better food, but for feeding on nothing else. Truth has been sought in the wrong direction, and the attainable has been put aside for the visionary.[81]

The *Essay* of 1845 had treated religious doctrine only from the point of view of logical development, and a more vigorous exposition of the logical cogency of faith was needed to demonstrate to the modern mind that it is reasonable to accept certain acts of assent which transcend logic and that religious knowledge can be just as objective and scientific as secular knowledge. As a result of this recognition, the idea of a *Grammar of Assent* emerged and developed in Newman's mind. The actual writing "on a subject which has teazed me for these twenty or thirty years" began in 1866 while he was vacationing in Switzerland.[82] Negotiations regarding the Oxford oratory interrupted his work in 1867; but, by the summer of 1868, he had nearly completed the first draft.

On July 2, 1869, Newman began sending proof sheets to Dr. Charles Meynell, Professor of Philosophy at Oscott. Meynell had expressed admiration for the Oxford University sermons on faith and reason, and Newman requested his criticisms of the *Grammar of Assent*. Meynell supplied valuable suggestions especially as to the precise meaning of philosophical terms; and, upon the book's completion, Newman gratefully wrote to him: "What the positive value of my volume is I do not know; but this I do know, that, many as are its imperfections and faults, they would have been many more and much worse but for you." [83] The final work on the book was done in January, 1870, and Newman received the first printed copy on February 21, his sixty-ninth birthday.

An eminent theologian and authority on Newman considers the *Grammar of Assent* as "the most difficult to summarize" of all his works; for "every detail, every tiny illustrative point we eliminate, turns out, to our surprise, to have been indispensable to the general effect." [84] Newman's terminology, moreover, is distinctively his own; although he uses many terms peculiar to certain philosophers, he gives them slightly different meanings.[85]

Newman divided his work into two parts: assent and apprehension, and assent and inference. At the end of each part he applies the conclusions to matters of religion. He calls upon the basic grammatical structure of a sentence—subject and predicate

—to demonstrate the distinction between assent and apprehension. In any statement or proposition "one term is predicated of another; the subject is referred to the predicate, and the predicate gives us information about the subject;—therefore to apprehend the proposition is to have the information, and to assent to it is to acquiesce in it as true." [86] Of the two components of the proposition, the predicate requires apprehension; the subject need not necessarily be apprehended for genuine assent. The subject in itself is unknown; it becomes known through the predicate.[87] The apprehension is "real" when the predicate expresses things external to the reader; "notional," when it expresses his thoughts or ideas.[88] Assent is readily given to real apprehension, for "it is in human nature to be more affected by the concrete than by the abstract," and "the reality of the thesis is almost a condition of its unconditionality." [89] Notional apprehension is always preceded by inference, which is composed of argument and conclusion; assent is had when the conclusion is accepted.[90] Inference, however, is at first conditional; conclusions are only tentatively held, subject to additional investigation.[91]

In religious matters, Newman fully realized that the mind desires certitude, "a consciousness of being right." [92] For "without certitude in religious faith there may be much decency of profession and of observance, but there can be no habit of prayer, no directness of devotion, no intercourse with the unseen, no generosity of self-sacrifice." [93] Certitude is readily had from the self-evident data of real apprehension, but the problem is how the mind passes from a conditional inference to certitude. In this instance, Newman made a contribution to religious thought. As in non-religious matters the mind, in accepting the generalizations of science and the great outlines of history, is guided by probabilities founded on certainties,[94] so the mind is guided in religious affairs by a method described as "the cumulation of probabilities, independent of each other, arising out of the nature and circumstances of the particular case which is under review; probabilities too fine to avail separately, too subtle and circuitous to be convertible into syllogisms, too numerous and various for such conversion, even were they convertible." [95] The ability of the human mind to discover certitude in a mass of converging probabilities is termed by Newman "the illative sense"—the human mind judging and correlating, or analyzing and synthesizing principles, doctrines, facts, testimonies, memories, experiences, and proceeding to "an accumulation of probabilities . . . and from probabilities we may construct legitimate proof, sufficient for certitude." [96]

Newman's *Grammar* created a varied reaction. The Jesuit, Thomas Harper, attacked it as contrary to the traditional method of Scholasticism which emphasized the evidence of design in the world as an argument for the existence of God.[97] Newman, instead, stressed the role of conscience as having the ability to arrive at an apprehension of God from an early age; "the child," he points out, "keenly understands that there is a difference between right and wrong, he is conscious that he is offending One to whom he is amenable, whom he does not see, who sees him. His mind reaches forward with a strong presentiment to the thought of a Moral Governor, sovereign over him, mindful and just. It comes to him like an impulse of nature to entertain it." [98]

Replying to William R. Brownlow, who had written to him concerning the blatant omission of design as proof for God's existence, Newman pointed out that he had referred to the argument from design, "order implies purpose";[99] but he explained, "I have not insisted on the argument from *design*, because I am writing for the nineteenth century, by which, as represented by its philosophers, design is not admitted as proved. And to tell the truth, . . . I have been unable to see the logical force of the argument myself. I believe in design because I believe in God; not in God because I see design. . . . Half the world knows nothing of the argument from design—and, when you have got it, you do not prove by it the moral attributes of God—except very faintly. Design teaches me power, skill, and goodness, not sanctity, not mercy, not a future judgment, which three are of the essence of religion." [100]

Conscience, for Newman, has "a legitimate place among our mental acts"; for, while reliance upon sensible phenomena provides the basis from which to reason to God's existence, reliance upon mental phenomena can lead to belief in a Creator. Or as Newman delineated:

As from a multitude of instinctive perceptions, acting in particular instances, of something beyond the senses, we generalize the notion of an external world, and then picture that world in and according to those particular phenomena from which we started, *so* from the perceptive power which identifies the intimations of conscience with the reverberations or echoes (so to say) of an external admonition, we proceed on to the notion of a Supreme Ruler and Judge, and then again we image Him and His attributes in those recurring intimations, out of which, as mental phenomena, our recognition of His existence was originally gained.[101]

Inanimate objects lack the power of conscience, which arouses feelings of fear, shame, and responsibility. Inanimate objects lead to a logical conclusion of God as a principle or a cause, but conscience views God as a person; and men living in accord with conscience "are brought into His presence as that of a Living Person, and are able to hold converse with Him, and that with a directness and simplicity, with a confidence and intimacy, *mutatis mutandis*, which we use towards an earthly superior; so that it is doubtful whether we realize the company of our fellow-men with greater keenness than these favoured minds are able to contemplate and adore the Unseen, Incomprehensible Creator." [102]

To Newman's suprise, William G. Ward, often at odds with him on many issues, enthusiastically praised the *Grammar* in the conservative *Dublin Review*. Ward demonstrated that Newman was not only in the mainstream of Scholasticism and orthodoxically sound but that his argument from conscience met the religious needs of the day.[103] Ward's defence of Newman served much to undo Harper's opposition; subsequently, the *Grammar* has been widely read and accepted. A more recent evaluation of the *Grammar* places it as "the first great attempt to give a defence of Christian faith in a language that allowed, recognised and answered the lack of faith in the modern world, . . . because in it Newman, rejecting the purely intellectualist approach to the problem of God, talks a language . . . much more like that of the modern analyst and existentialist." [104] Cronin, however, in studying Newman's theory of knowledge, demonstrates that "in all major points" it "can be harmonized with the philosophy of Aristotle, St. Thomas, and the neo-scholastics." [105]

VI *Papal Infallibility*

At the age of sixty-nine Newman expected the *Grammar of Assent* to be his last work. But he who could not write and publish "without a *call*" [106] was to receive such a call from none other than William E. Gladstone, for many years leader of the Liberals in the English Parliament. In November, 1874, Gladstone published *The Vatican Decrees and Their Bearing on Civil Allegiance* —an attack on the position of Vatican Council I on the infallibility of the Pope. Gladstone unequivocally maintained that the Council's definition of the infallibility prerogative exacted a loyalty on the part of Roman Catholics that would be inconsistent with loyalty to civil authority.

Gladstone's position was not without justification. Pope Pius IX had condemned—in his encyclical, *Quanta Cura* and in an accompanying document entitled *Syllabus of Errors,* both issued in 1864—modern liberal ideas of extreme individualism and of the supremacy of the civil authority over the ecclesiastical. The Pope, furthermore, had convened in 1869 a general council of the Catholic Church, whose definition of papal supremacy and infallibility had engendered anti-clerical campaigns in France, Italy, and Spain, and contributed to the success of the *Kulturkampf* in the rising nationalism of Germany. And there were Roman Catholics, known at Ultramontanes, who had been active in promoting a strong position for the Pope.

Ardent exponents of Ultramontanism in England were Cardinal Manning, Archbishop of Westminster since 1865, and William G. Ward.[107] Although converts from Anglicanism, they were antagonizing their fellow Englishmen and causing alarm by their extreme stand. They equated liberalism with heresy and favored "maximizing" Catholic doctrine—the Catholic Church was to determine clearly and fully what they had to hold as loyal Roman Catholics.[108] Manning, moreover, had recently published a lecture entitled, "Caesarism and Ultramontanism," which portrayed an endless, feverish struggle between the Pope and civil authority: allegiance to either "Peter" or "Caesar" was the inevitable dichotomy.

Newman, therefore, saw in Gladstone's publication an occasion not only for answering the false charges on the part of non-Catholics but also for rectifying the exaggerations of papal supremacy and infallibility on the part of some of his fellow English Catholics, with whom he had been annoyed about this point for some time. Since Gladstone had not directed his pamphlet to him, Newman preferred not to answer Gladstone directly; instead, Newman chose the Duke of Norfolk to whom he could address a public letter. The Duke, who belonged to an old English family which had long been known for its loyalty to the Roman Catholic Church and to the British Crown alike, was one of the many who had urged Newman to a rebuttal of Gladstone's arguments. Since the Duke of Norfolk was also the leading Roman Catholic in the British government at the time, the question of civil and spiritual allegiance concerned him vitally.[109] The *Letter to the Duke of Norfolk* is approximately two hundred pages in length; its complete title is *A Letter to His Grace the Duke of Norfolk on Occasion of Mr. Gladstone's Recent Expostulation;* and it was issued in the middle of January, 1875, having been completed on December 27, 1874.

With logical analysis and historical documentation, Newman answers each of Gladstone's charges. His aim is to offer a clear and objective presentation of papal infallibility, which proves the "extraordinary severity" of Gladstone's allegations as "neither trustworthy nor charitable" and "the chronic extravagances of knots of Catholics here and there . . . who have stated truths in the most paradoxical form." [110]

All of Newman's arguments revolve around two main considerations: the proper sphere of papal infallibility and freedom of conscience. Realizing that, without a correct notion of the papal prerogative as defined by Vatican Council I, false interpretations could be easily rendered, Newman emphasizes that the Council primarily set restrictions on the exercise of infallibility. The Pope can speak with infallible authority only on matters of faith and morals in his role as the Catholic Church's Universal Teacher as determined by Christ's power granted to Peter and so understood by nineteen hundred years of practice in the church's history. The Pope, furthermore, must clearly announce the use of this prerogative and intend his decision to be binding on all members of the church. His infallibility does not extend to his personal and private life and thought, nor to his decisions as a temporal ruler or governor of the church.[111]

As for a Roman Catholic's freedom of conscience in view of the Pope's teaching prerogative, infallibility is a judgment on speculative truth or abstract doctrine, while conscience bears immediately on conduct, on something to be done or not done; it is a "practical dictate." [112] Infallibility does not embrace a "minute supervision" of everything that one does. "The Pope is not infallible in that subject-matter in which conscience is of supreme authority," [113] for conscience is a "dutiful obedience to what claims to be a divine voice, speaking within us." [114] But Newman strongly insists that conscience must not be "a long-sighted selfishness"—"the right of thinking, speaking, writing, and acting according to one's judgment . . . , without any thought of God at all," or a "miserable counterfeit" that can be classified as "license" or "self-will." [115] As a "stern monitor," conscience avails itself of serious thought, prayer, and all available means of arriving at a right judgment on a matter in question.[116] Circumstances would be rare, indeed, when a Pope's general proposition or condemnation of a particular error would conflict with an individual's conscience.[117]

As to a possible conflict of a Roman Catholic's loyalty to his country, a cardinal objection of Gladstone, Newman clarifies by means of examples. If Parliament enacted a law requiring attendance at Protestant services for all Englishmen, the Roman Catholic would be bound in conscience to obey the Pope's regulation and not the civil law's. On the other hand, if the Pope were to ask all Catholic military men to withdraw from service to their country, then Newman would feel free in conscience to disobey the Pope's command.[118]

The reply to Gladstone produced an immediate response of approval on the part of all Englishmen, and Newman expressed great pleasure at its success. Of particular note was Ward's cordial acceptance of it in the *Dublin Review*.[119] What Newman enunciated nearly one hundred years ago has been reiterated by the Catholic Church's Vatican Council II in its "Dogmatic Constitution of the Church" (1964), "Pastoral Constitution on the Church in the Modern World" (1965), and the "Declaration on Religious Freedom—On the Right of the Person and of Communities to Social and Civil Freedom in Matters Religious" (1965).[120]

The *Letter to the Duke of Norfolk* was Newman's last work. He initiated no new literary project; instead, he employed his time in revising earlier works, most notably, *An Essay on the Development of Christian Doctrine* and *Tracts for the Times*. The former work underwent a thorough rearrangement and enlargement of the text; its basic thesis, however, remained intact. But in the *Tracts* Newman the Anglican had delineated his famous *Via Media*—the position which placed the Anglican Church between the extremes of Roman Catholicism's constantly adding to the original body of divine truth and Protestantism's gradual elimination of teachings from it. Having left Anglicanism for Roman Catholicism, Newman in 1877 regarded it as a matter of duty to truth to retract his previous statements. He does not, as might be expected, absolve the Church of Rome of all the charges he had hurled against her forty years before; instead, he asks, "What line of conduct, except on the long, the very long run, is at once edifying, expedient, and true?" [121] For Newman, firm in his belief in the Catholic Church as divinely instituted, had to acknowledge that it was entrusted for its government to human beings. He distinguished—unlike lofty idealists—between a "divine" church and a "human" church:

All this was foreseen certainly by the Divine Mind, when He committed to His Church so complex a mission; and, by promising her infallibility in her formal teaching, He indirectly protected her from serious error in worship and political action also. This aid, however, great as it is, does not secure her from all dangers as regards the problem which she has to solve; nothing but the gift of impeccability granted to her authorities would secure them from all liability to mistake in their conduct, policy, words and decisions, in her legislative and her executive, in ecclesiastical and disciplinarian details; and such a gift they have not received. In consequence, however well she may perform her duties on the whole, it will always be easy for her enemies to make a case against her, well founded or not, from the action or interaction, or the chronic collisions or contrasts, or the temporary suspense or delay, of her administration, in her three several departments of duty,—her government, her devotions, and her schools,— from the conduct of her rulers, her divines, her pastors, or her people.[122]

Newman, furthermore, admitted that the *Via Media* was merely the "dressing up of an hypothesis" that had been devised in the absence of direct proof.[123] He felt no need to dwell on his Anglican charge that the modern Church of Rome had lost its continuity with primitive Christianity, for the *Essay on Development* had as its *raison d'être* the task of proving the logical continuity.[124] He saw, moreover, an extension of development in the flexibility of the Catholic Church to adjust herself to varied races, nationalities, and circumstances of place and time.[125]

VII   *Singular Honors*

The death of one of Newman's closest friends, Ambrose St. John, occurred in 1875. It was a great personal loss, and he frequently wrote to other friends of the thirty-two years that St. John had stood by him in the most turbulent periods of his life.[126] Especially did Newman wish St. John at his side in the years of melancholy loneliness of old age, but more particularly he desired him to rejoice with him in the singular honors of which he was to be the recipient. In 1878, Newman's alma mater at Oxford, Trinity College, elected him its first Honorary Fellow. He regarded the honor as "a great compliment, perhaps the greatest I have ever received." It was at Trinity that he had been an undergraduate from the age of sixteen to twenty-one, and with warm sentiment he expressed his gratitude for the honor and the anticipation of returning to "the place where I began the battle of life." [127]

The election of Cardinal Pecci as Pope Leo XIII after the death of Pius IX in 1878 led to the bestowal of another singular honor. It became readily apparent that the new pontiff was considering the promotion of Newman to cardinal of the Roman Catholic Church. The Duke of Norfolk, England's leading Catholic layman, had suggested the honor in a personal visit to the Pope in Rome.[128] When Newman was informed early in 1879 of the impending honor through Bishop Ullathorne, he regarded the cardinalate as "altogether above me" but "quite transcendent and unparalleled." He felt he could not refuse but had to entreat "compassion" for being asked to leave, in feeble health at the age of seventy-nine, his native England for Rome; he intimated in his letter to Ullathorne the possibility of remaining in England.[129] By the middle of March, 1879, the official appointment of Newman to the cardinalate was announced, with the privilege of continuing residence at his oratory in England.[130] He did undertake the arduous journey to Rome to receive personally the "red hat" in a special ceremony on May 12.

Newman's elevation to a prince of the Roman Catholic Church served as the climax to a life devoted to the scholarly pursuit of religious and secular truth. The charges, accusations, and innuendoes that beset him many times in his life seemed to have vanished completely. As he remarked to his fellow Oratorians, "The cloud is lifted from me forever." Many in England felt strongly that Leo

XIII had honored Newman "not merely as a Catholic but also as a great Englishman, . . . as an honour to England." [131] Manning was personally told by the Pope that the elevation was a testimony to Newman's virtues and learning.[132] The English, Irish, Scotch, and American residents in Rome, in their official greetings to the newly robed cardinal, summed up the affectionate esteem held by so many throughout the world: "We feel that in making you a Cardinal the Holy Father has not only given public testimony of his appreciation of your great merits and of the value of your admirable writings in defence of God and His Church, but also conferred the greatest possible honour on all English-speaking Catholics who have long looked up to you as their spiritual father and their guide in the paths of holiness." [133]

Newman's return to England was followed by many receptions, but he longed for quiet and solitude. He retired to the Birmingham Oratory to utilize his remaining years in revising his writings, in translating them into Latin, and in corresponding with friends. Although Newman intended no other publications, discussions in 1883 about the inspiration of Sacred Scripture convinced him that the question needed reconsideration. In November, 1883, he presented to the periodical, *Nineteenth Century*, an essay on inspiration which was published in the February, 1884, issue. Newman, who rejected the fundamentalist position that the Bible was literally inspired, maintained that such a position justified the modernist's denial of inspiration because the Bible contained so many statements and facts contrary to the discoveries of science. As Newman distinguished them, the truths of faith and morals come within the province of divine inspiration; but the literary style of the human writer, with his descriptions of nature (or *obiter dicta*, as Newman called them), were not necessarily inspired.[134] His views antedated by ten years Leo XIII's encyclical on the study of Scripture, "Providentissimus Deus," as well as present-day trends in Biblical scholarship.

In 1885, still another, but the last, duty to write came to Newman. Writing in the *Contemporary Review* of May, 1885, on "Catholicism and Religious Thought," Principal Fairbairn, a Congregationalist minister, singled out Newman: "He has a deep distrust of the intellect; he dares not trust his own, for he does not know where it might lead him, and he will not trust any other man's." Of the *Grammar of Assent*, Fairbairn remarked, "The book is pervaded by the intensest philosophical scepticism." [135] In Newman's reply in the article "The Development of Religious Error," in the October issue of the same periodical, he emphasized that human reason can be led astray by many false ideologies; but the Roman Catholic Church, as the custodian of divine truth, seeks to guide mankind and guard it against the corrupting influences of the irreligious. Reason must never be unbridled; it needs direction—from religious faith and the established church. [136]

Newman's last years saw a considerable curtailing of his few activities, including the writing of letters, which he now dictated. He preached his last sermon on January 1, 1888, on the occasion of the celebration of Leo XIII's golden jubilee in the priesthood. The physical powers of the eighty-nine-year-old cardinal gradually diminished; and he died of lung congestion on August 11, 1890. He was buried on August 18 at Rednal; and, in accordance with his request, he was placed next to the grave of his dearest friend, Ambrose St. John. His memorial epitaph, engraved on the tombstone, was also of his choosing: *Ex umbris et imaginibus in veritatem*—"From shadows and images unto truth." Truth was both his earthly and celestial goal.

CHAPTER 6

The Legacy of Newman

THE legacy of John Henry Newman to posterity can be said to be threefold: as a writer, as a thinker, and as a man. In each of these three aspects of his contribution, he made an ever-lasting imprint on those who have read and studied him. His is a legacy relevant to an age that needs guidance to grapple with problems requiring steadfast devotion to truth, an uncompromising attitude toward error, and an equilibrium characterized by charity and forbearance in combating error.

I   The Writer

Few men of letters have been as versatile as Newman in employing diverse modes of expression. He is poet, letter writer, preacher, novelist, research scholar, essayist, historian, philosopher. Other Victorian writers in English literature may be more renowned for a particular mode of literary expression—Robert Browning and Alfred, Lord Tennyson in poetry; Thomas Macaulay and Thomas Carlyle in historical writing; Robert Louis Stevenson and Charles Dickens in the writing of novels; John Ruskin and Matthew Arnold for their essays; John Stuart Mill and Herbert Spencer in philosophy: but Newman surpasses all of them in the versatility of literary media chosen.

It could be asked what determined Newman's mode of expression. Style for style's sake was not his criterion. The message or truth to be expounded determined his style. He practiced what he preached: the thoughts and reasonings of an author have a personal character; "his style is not only the image of his subject, but of his mind":[1]

The Art of Letters is the method by which a speaker or writer brings out in words, worthy of his subject, and sufficient for his audience or readers, the thoughts that impress him. Literature, then, is of a personal character; it consists in the enunciations and teachings of those who have a right to speak as representatives of their kind, and in whose words their brethren find an interpretation of their own sentiments, a record of their own experience, and a suggestion for their own judgments. A great author . . . is not one who merely has a *copia verborum,* whether in prose or verse, and can, as it were, turn on at his will any number of splendid phrases and swelling sentences; but he is one who has something to say and knows how to say it.[2]

He writes passionately, because he feels keenly; forcibly, because he conceives vividly; he sees too clearly to be vague; he is too serious to be otiose; he can analyze his subject, and therefore he is rich; he embraces it as a whole and in its parts, and therefore he is consistent; he has a firm hold of it, and therefore is luminous. When his imagination wells up, it overflows in ornament; when his heart is touched, it thrills along his verse. He always has the right word for the right idea, and never a word too much. If he is brief, it is because few words suffice; when he is lavish of them, still each word has its mark, and aids, not embarrasses, the vigorous march of his elocution. He expresses what all feel, but all cannot say; and his sayings pass into proverbs among his people, and his phrases become household words and idioms of their daily speech, which is tesselated with the rich fragments of his language, as we see in foreign lands the marbles of Roman grandeur worked into the walls and pavements of modern palaces.[3]

Although Newman subordinated style to thought, he was painstakingly scrupulous in producing his manuscripts. With the exception of the *Apologia*—for which he had weekly deadlines to meet—he was known for revising and re-revising all that he wrote. For this reason, vivid exactness is considered the essence of Newman's style.[4] It was Newman himself who had preached, "Words have a meaning, whether we intend that meaning or not." [5] A devotion to truth, to a cause, would permit neither deliberate distortion of facts nor poorly chosen words that could becloud or confuse the true meaning of facts.

With all Newman's rigid adherence to exactness, he did not offer readers and hearers a sterile message; for vividness in style accompanied exactness. His was a psychological insight into the minds and hearts of the people to whom he addressed his message. Before setting down his thoughts in writing, it seemed that he had already before him a psychological case study of his hearers:

their feelings, conflicts, prejudices. His opening lecture to the Irish for the establishment of a university is a masterpiece of psychological insight into the conflicting opinions about university education. His lectures to non-Catholics begin with a common denominator of belief. His poems, "Lead Kindly Light" and *Dream of Gerontius,* are the outpouring of his own heart, but they are irresistible to the hearts of others who share similar hopes and fears. His *Apologia* produces an immediate compassion for the unjust attacks hurled against his own personal sincerity and against the cause he represented.

As his motto stated—*Cor ad cor loquitur* (Heart speaks to heart)—Newman always spoke from the heart to the heart, as well as from the mind to the mind. And with a realization that, if he sought to move a person's emotions, the emotional change was to be a result primarily of an intellectual conviction. Where the appeal to the mind is basically objective truth, the appeal to the emotions is one of candid sincerity. The skillful use of literary style affords the vehicle of appeal to both the heart and the mind. Newman's own words undoubtedly express this point with greater brilliance:

If then the power of speech is a gift as great as any that can be named, —if the origin of language is by many philosophers even considered to be nothing short of divine,—if by means of words the secrets of the heart are brought to light, pain of soul is relieved, hidden grief is carried off, sympathy conveyed, counsel imparted, experience recorded, and wisdom perpetuated,—if by great authors the many are drawn up into unity, national character is fixed, a people speaks, the past and the future, the East and the West are brought into communication with each other,—if such men are, in a word, the spokesmen and prophets of the human family,—it will not answer to make light of Literature or to neglect its study; rather we may be sure that, in proportion as we master it in whatever language, and imbibe its spirit, we shall ourselves become in our own measure the ministers of like benefits to others, be they many or few, be they in the obscurer or the more distinguished walks of life,—who are united to us by social ties, and are within the sphere of our personal influence.[6]

It is no wonder that Reilly, in his study of Newman as a man of letters, concluded that "no other prose writer of his century has invaded the world of subjective things with senses as alert as his nor more completely realized in his own work his conception of the power and dignity of literature." [7]

But it is in the evaluation of Newman the preacher that is found one of the strongest testimonies to Newman the writer. As a result of her study of Victorian literature, Amy Cruse concluded that "a congregation could offer no higher compliment to its pastor than a request that his sermon or sermons be published." [8] Newman's sermons have been published, not because of their manner of delivery, but principally for their content; for his fame as a preacher did not rest on oratorical ability. [9] A contemporary description of Newman the preacher was rendered in the *Dublin Review:*

Action in the common sense of the word there was none. Through many [of his sermons] the preacher never moved anything but his head. His hands were literally not seen from the beginning to the end. The sermon began in a calm musical voice, the key slightly rising as it went on; by-and-bye the preacher warmed with his subject, it seemed as if his very soul and body glowed with suppressed emotion. There were times when, in the midst of the most thrilling passages, he would pause, without dropping his voice, for a moment which seemed long, before he uttered with gathering force and solemnity a few weighty words. [10]

As to answer to the secret of Newman the preacher, it may be found in his own essay on "University Preaching"; in it, he un-equivocally states that "one thing is necessary,—an intense per-ception and appreciation of the end for which he preaches, and that is, to be the minister of some definite spiritual good to those who hear him." [11] Although the oratorical qualities of voice modu-lation, gesticulation, and dramatic suspense may serve as requi-sites for the "perfection" of a preacher, Newman subordinated them to the primary goal of preaching; for, as the Apostle Paul wrote, "The kingdom of God is not in speech, but in power." [12]

Furthermore, Newman classifies "a resolution to be eloquent" as an "impediment to persuasion." The primary goal of preaching is achieved through earnestness brought about by an intellectual conviction of presenting some definite spiritual good in the mes-sage, one worthy of communicating to others. [13] Although over-shadowed by his contemporaries for oratorical skill, "Newman alone is read widely today as a master of sermon eloquence." [14]

The devotees of a Classical education can appeal to Newman for support. Although he admitted copying the style of Addison at fourteen or fifteen, writing in the style of Johnson and being impressed with the cadence of the sentences of Gibbon at seventeen, he wrote at sixty-eight: "The only master of style I have ever had is Cicero. I think I owe a great deal to him, but as far as I know, to no one else. His great mastery of Latin is shown especially in his clearness." [15] For of Cicero he also noted: "His copious, majestic, musical flow of language, even if sometimes beyond what the subject-matter demands, is never out of keeping with the occasion or with the speaker. It is the expression of lofty sentiments in lofty sentences, the *mens magna in corpore magno*. It is the development of the inner man." [16]

II   *The Thinker*

In the present-day cult of modernity, with its disdain for the past, few men have achieved contemporary relevancy. Newman's thought is relevant today, and it gives strength to Giovanni Costigan's claim for the nineteenth-century writer and thinker as "a force of individual genius in history." [17] Indeed, hardly any humanist educator has failed to quote Newman's *Idea of a University*. The mania for specialization, with its consequent result of narrow-mindedness and inability to communicate with those not of the same intellectual discipline, has led to a greater awareness of the necessity for a liberal education, which Newman so ably portrayed. Numerous leading American educators have enunciated Newman's thought: Robert Maynard Hutchins, Abraham Flexner, Mark Van Doren, Mortimer Adler. In a call for the integration of knowledge today, Arthur Bestor reflects forcefully the *Idea of a University* in his challenge to the times: "To restore to intellectual life the unity that the forces of modern life are threatening to destroy constitutes one of the most significant tasks to which thoughtful men and women are addressing themselves today." [18] Both Catholic and Protestant educational humanists would reason even further with Newman and call upon the study of theology as the central, unifying force of the curriculum. Christopher Dawson possibly best expresses this view when he asks for theology to be not as "a kind of extra insecurely tacked on to the general educational structure," but as "a principle of cultural unity and as the creator of moral values." [19]

Newman's influence in religious thought today is paramount. In the Roman Catholic Church's recent Vatican Council II, it was frequently commented that "this is Cardinal Newman's Council." [20] He was, moreover, believed to be cited more often than any of the other thinkers on the issues discussed, including St. Thomas Aquinas, the philosopher and theologian *par excellence* of Roman Catholicism for many centuries.[21] In calling an ecumenical council, Pope John XXIII quoted from Newman's *Difficulties felt by Anglicans* in support for the church's need for *aggiornamento* or updating: "There are quite a number of points which the Catholic Church leaves to the discussion of theologians, both in so far as these points are not absolutely certain, and also, in so far as controversies of this kind do not tear asunder the unity of the Church, but rather greatly contribute (by striking new light out of the friction of the various opinions) to a deeper and better understanding of the dogmas, and level and strengthen the path to the attainment of that unity." [22] Pope Paul VI has extolled Newman as "that remarkable mind . . . who . . . guided solely by love of the truth and fidelity to Christ, traced an itinerary, the most toilsome, but also the greatest, the most meaningful, the most conclusive, that human thought ever travelled during the last century, indeed one might say during the modern era, to arrive at the fulness of wisdom and of peace." [23] Outstanding present-day Roman Catholic theologians have quoted Newman frequently.[24] Catholic bishops, in their speeches at the Council, cited him as authority for their views.[25]

Among the issues discussed and voted upon at the Council were the collegiality of bishops, the role of the laity, and freedom of conscience. Newman had voiced his opinions, now substantially accepted in the twentieth century, some one hundred years previously. Opposed to the extremist position on papal infallibility in 1870, Newman declined an invitation to attend Vatican Council I. He considered the extension of infallibility to every utterance of the Pope, including specifically encyclicals, to be an exaggeration and an unwise hindrance to ecumenism.[26] Although Vatican Council I did not accept this extremist view, but set forth a more moderate position with definite limits on the extent of papal infallibility, Newman had hoped for, then predicted, that the role of the bishops in sharing the prerogatives of infallibility would be later clarified. Vatican Council II, in its epochal "Dogmatic Constitution of the Church," fulfilled Newman's hope and prophecy of collegiality of bishops and Pope in both the ruling and the teaching authority in the Catholic Church.[27]

Accepted also by Vatican Council II are Newman's views on an expanding and more prominent role for the laity in church affairs, extending to the laity positions of leadership and administration in all spheres of the church's apostolic endeavors.[28] Freedom of conscience in religious matters, urged by Newman when few men dared proclaim such a "subversive" doctrine, has become a cardinal principle of Roman Catholicism since Vatican Council II.[29]

It is not only for the issues *qua* issues that Vatican Council II is indebted to Newman; it is also for the reasoning process whereby issues are resolved, so strongly does contemporary theological thought reflect the mind of the nineteenth-century English theologian. The idea of development of doctrine, as thought out by Newman in his days of transition from Anglicanism to Roman Catholicism, has made an imprint upon today's theological thinking. The American Jesuit theologian, John Courtney Murray, typified development of doctrine as "*the* issue underlying all issues at the Council." [30] Pope John's call to update did not imply any radical change of church dogmas and procedures but a presentation of these dogmas and procedures in a manner better understood and more meaningful to the mind of the twentieth century. As far back as 1867 the French theologian Félix Ravaisson wrote that "perhaps a time will come in which the idea of development will prevail in religion, no less than in any science. For example, the eminent Catholic doctor, Mr. Newman, has set forth such an idea, which wins over more minds from day to day." [31] Vatican Council II perceived this need for development.

Crises of thought within the Roman Catholic Church today have been caused by extremists: those desirous of change for change's sake; those adamantly opposed to change of any kind. To these extremists Newman offers a new *via media*—a position of developmentalism from old to new, a position rooted in the rich, spiritual heritage of the past, yet permitted to develop with vigor in a changing world with new vistas, new perspectives, new findings from all intellectual pursuits. Neither conservatism nor liberalism but developmentalism would be Newman's guide to the contemporary mind's search for truth.[32] A *Credo in Newmanum,* once voiced so enthusiastically by young followers and admirers at Oxford, would be a practical guide to those engaged in the *aggiornamento* of Roman Catholicism today.

III *The Man*

The legacy of most authors to mankind lies in their writings and thought. For some, their deeds and personality surpass the impact and message of their writings. In the case of Newman, mankind has been left a literary heritage coupled with the record of an equally forceful personality that attracted men to him and that made itself felt in the sequence of historical events. The *London Quarterly Review*, in commenting on the effect of his religious conversion, said that "we pretend not to disguise or to undervalue the loss sustained by the Church of England in a man of his piety, ability, and influence; such a loss perhaps has not been experienced since the Reformation." [33]

Newman's magnetic quality of leadership was recognized in his Oxford days. James Anthony Froude, the brother of Hurrell, has described vividly the impression that Newman was creating:

Clever men were looking with interest and curiosity on the apparition among them of one of those persons of indisputable genius who was likely to make a mark upon his time. . . . There was an original force of character which refused to be moulded by circumstances, which was to make its own way, and become a power in the world; a clearness of intellectual perception, a disdain for conventionalities, a temper imperious and wilful, but along with it a most attracting gentleness, sweetness, singleness of heart and purpose. . . . I had then never seen so impressive a person. I met him now and then in private; I attended his church and heard him preach Sunday after Sunday; he is supposed to have been insidious, to have led his disciples on to conclusions to which he designed to bring them, while his purpose was carefully veiled. He was, on the contrary, the most transparent of men. He told us what he believed to be true. He did not know where it would carry him. No one who has ever risen to any great height in this world refuses to move till he knows where he is going. He is impelled in each step which he takes by a force within himself. He satisfies himself only that the step is a right one, and he leaves the rest to Providence. Newman's mind was world-wide. He was interested in everything which was going on in science, in politics, in literature. Nothing was too large for him, nothing too trivial, if it threw light upon the central question, what man really was, and what was his destiny. . . . He could admire enthusiastically any greatness of action and character, however remote the sphere of it from his own.

   With us undergraduates, Newman . . . spoke to us about subjects of the day, of literature, of public persons and incidents, of everything which was generally interesting. He seemed always to be better informed on common topics of conversation than anyone else who was present. He was never condescending with us, never didactic or authoritative; but what he said carried conviction with it. When we were wrong, he knew why we were wrong, and excused our mistakes to ourselves while he set us right. Perhaps his supreme merit as a talker was that he never tried to be witty or to say striking things. Ironical he could be, but not ill-natured. Not a malicious anecdote was ever heard from him. Prosy he could not be. He was lightness itself—the lightness of elastic strength—and he was interesting because he never talked for talking's sake, but because he had something real to say.

   Thus it was that we, who had never seen such another man, and to whom he appeared, perhaps, at special advantage in contrast with the normal college don, came to regard Newman with the affection of pupils (though pupils, strictly speaking, he had none) for an idolized master. The simplest word which dropped from him was treasured as if it had been an intellectual diamond.[34]

   Despite James Froude's description of a keen mind vitally concerned in the panorama of life's problems, a few writers have accused Newman of being unmoved by the great social problems of his day. "All these left him unstirred," remarks Harrold.[35] Herbert Stewart, in his *A Century of Anglo-Catholicism*, rebukes Newman for lack of involvement: "The famine in Ireland, the vast selfishness of the Corn Laws, Chartism, the opium war in China —how a Hebrew prophet would have dealt with them! But one would gather from Newman's sermons that the social passion of an Isaiah or a Jeremiah had no place in Christianity." [36] E. B. Burgum, seeking to convince the reader of the restrictiveness of Newman's range of intellectual thought, has written: "There was no writer of the period who wrote with a more complete unconsciousness of their existence [social problems] in state or church." [37]

   But Newman, although scholarly and introspective by nature, was aware of the world about him, as the following statement indicates: "What largeness of view, what intrepidity, vigor, and resolution are implied in the Reform Bill, in the Emancipation of the Blacks, in the finance changes, in the Useful Knowledge movement, in the organization of the Free Kirk, in the introduction of the penny postage, and in the railroads! This is an age, if not of great men, at least of great works." [38]

Possibly, Newman was his own worst enemy; as he emphasized so poignantly in his spiritual autobiography, he was the victim of a "mistrust of the reality of material phenomena, . . . making me rest in the thought of two, and two only, absolute and luminously self-evident beings—myself and my Creator;—for while I considered myself predestined to salvation, my mind did not dwell upon others, as fancying them simply passed over, not predestined to eternal death. I only thought of the mercy to myself." [39] But it must be admitted that his concern was with the most basic problem: man and his relation to God. Newman dedicated his life to bring Everyman closer to God, as his words and his example attest. His life was not that of the ivory-tower clergyman or educator. Men today *feel* with him in the spiritual struggle delineated in the *Apologia*. He has disciples in religious thought today who echo his views and his spirit for a free mind in a free church. His sermons are quoted by preachers who wish to communicate the loftiest thoughts of man's aspiration towards God.

It is not surprising, therefore, that many Roman Catholics today are urging for Newman the highest honor that their church can bestow on mortal man—that of canonization as a saint. One such proponent has set forth the following case:

When studying his life and works, we are constantly impressed above all else with Newman's likeness to the Saints and Fathers of the Church. These similarities are manifest in every way—in the remarkable purity and holiness of his life, in the elevated quality of his mind and writings, . . . in the trials and anguish of soul that he endured, in the misunderstandings he occasioned, in the ardent friends that followed him and the bitter enemies that opposed him, in his vivid unwavering faith in God and things unseen and steadfast devotion to the truth as he saw it, in his total forgetfulness of self and wholehearted abandonment to the will of the Divine Master, whom to serve was the one grand passion of his life. . . . Add to these considerations the mighty influence for good throughout the world, which the great Cardinal exercised during his extended career, and the constant increase of that influence since his passing, and we can see that we have here not just another great scholar, or literary master, or unusual preacher, but a massive personality whose characteristics were: a vivid and constant awareness of the divine, moral and spiritual elevation, . . . entire detachment from the world and its prizes, oblivion of self and disregard for the esteem of men as such, and unabating strength in the pursuit of a goal which was God alone. The pursuit of holiness and personal sanctity was the preoccupation of his whole life, and the explanation of all he said and did.[40]

So the legacy of John Henry Newman as writer, thinker, and man —a saintly scholar and a scholarly saint.

Notes and References

Chapter One

1. For a genealogy of Newman's mother's family, see Wilfrid Ward, *The Life of John Henry Newman* (London, 1913), I, 615.
2. Harriet Mozley, *Family Adventures* (London, 1852).
3. Maisie Ward, *Young Mr. Newman* (New York, 1848), p. 4.
4. *Ibid.*, pp. 5–12.
5. Anne Mozley, ed., *Letters and Correspondence of John Henry Newman During His Life in the English Church, with a Brief Autobiography* (London, 1891), I, 36.
6. One biographer would go so far as to say that Newman "the boy was already a theologian even in his teens." Henry J. Jennings, *Cardinal Newman* (Birmingham, 1882), p. 7.
7. *Apologia pro Vita Sua*, ed. Maisie Ward (New York, 1946), p. 1.
8. A. Mozley, *Letters*, I, 22.
9. *Apologia*, pp. 1–2.
10. *Ibid.*, p. 2.
11. *Ibid.*, p. 3.
12. *Ibid.*, pp. 3–4.
13. *Ibid.*, p. 3.
14. H. P. Liddon, *Life of E. B. Pusey* (London, 1893–97), II, 450.
15. *Apologia*, pp. 4–5.
16. A. Mozley, *Letters*, I, 59.
17. *Apologia*, p. 5.
18. For a more complete view of Oxford in Newman's time, see Frank Leslie Cross, "Tractarian Oxford," in *John Henry Newman: with a Set of Unpublished Letters* (London, 1933); W. S. Knickerbocker, *Creative Oxford* (Syracuse, N. Y., 1925): Dean R. W. Church, *The Oxford Movement* (Hamden, Conn., 1966).
19. A. Mozley, *Letters*, I, 30; M. Ward, *Newman*, pp. 41–42.
20. Knickerbocker, *Creative Oxford*, pp. 32–34.
21. A. Mozley, *Letters*, I, 35.
22. *Ibid.*, p. 39.
23. *Ibid.*, p. 41.
24. *Ibid.*, p. 28.

25. M. Ward, *Newman*, pp. 46–47.
26. A. Mozley, *Letters*, I, 45.
27. *Ibid.*, p. 49.
28. *Ibid.*, p. 74.
29. *Ibid.*, p. 68.
30. *Ibid.*, p. 73.
31. *Ibid.*, p. 72.
32. *Ibid.*, p. 74.
33. *Ibid.*, p. 73.
34. *Ibid.*, pp. 105–06.
35. *Ibid.*, pp. 106–07.
36. *Ibid.*, p. 106.
37. Mark Pattison, *Memoirs* (London, 1885), p. 79.
38. *Apologia*, pp. 8–9.
39. *Ibid.*, pp. 6–7.
40. *Ibid.*, p. 7.
41. *Ibid.*, p. 9.
42. Newman to his sister Jemima, quoted from W. Ward, *Newman*, I, 41.
43. *Ibid.*
44. *Apologia*, pp. 10–11.
45. *Ibid.*, p. 11.
46. W. Ward, *Newman*, I, 42–43.
47. For a background of the Catholic Emancipation Act, see John J. O'Connor, *The Catholic Revival in England* (New York, 1942), pp. 1–29.
48. Newman to his mother, quoted from W. Ward, *Newman*, I, 44.
49. *Apologia*, p. 10.
50. *Ibid.*, p. 192.
51. *Ibid.*, p. 191.
52. *Essays Critical and Historical* (London, 1872), I, 34–35.
53. Charles Sarolea, *Cardinal Newman and His Influence on Religious Life and Thought* (Edinburgh, 1908), p. 150.
54. A. Mozley, *Letters*, I, 245.
55. *Sermons Preached on Various Occasions* (London, 1852), pp. 92–93.
56. A. Mozley, *Letters*, I, 254.
57. Sarolea, *Newman*, p. 77; William F. Barry, *Newman* (London, 1905), p. 42. For a discussion of the influence of the Greek Fathers of the Church and Platonism upon Newman, see Charles F. Harrold, "Newman and the Alexandrian Platonists," *Modern Philology*, XXXVII (1940), 279–91.
58. *The Arians of the Fourth Century* (London, 1833), p. 146.
59. *Ibid.*, p. 147.

60. Charles F. Harrold, *John Henry Newman* (London, 1945), p. 228.

61. Jean Guitton, *La philosophie de Newman: essai sur l'idée de développement* (Paris, 1933), pp. 2, 22.

62. A. Mozley, *Letters*, I, 265.

63. For Newman's own evaluation of Froude, see *Apologia*, pp. 15–17.

64. A. Mozley, *Letters*, I, 306–57.

65. *Ibid.*, pp. 358–79.

66. *Apologia*, p. 22.

67. *Ibid.*

68. *Ibid.*

69. *Verses on Various Occasions* (London, 1868), p. 92.

70. *Ibid.*, p. 97.

71. Richard H. Hutton, *Cardinal Newman* (London, 1891), p. 44.

72. *Apologia*, p. 23.

73. A. Mozley, *Letters*, I, 416–17.

74. *Ibid.*, p. 419.

75. *Verses*, p. 156.

Chapter Two

1. J. P. Stanley, *Life of Thomas Arnold, D.D.* (London, 1904), p. 278.

2. S. L. Ollard, *A Short History of the Oxford Movement* (London, 1915), p. 17.

3. D. C. Somervell, *English Thought in the Nineteenth Century* (New York, 1929), p. 17.

4. A. Mozley, *Letters*, I, 233.

5. See Thomas Carlyle's essay on "Sir Walter Scott," *Collected Works*, Vol. IV of *Critical and Miscellaneous Essays* (London, 1896–1899), p. 49.

6. *Apologia*, p. 23.

7. *Ibid.*, pp. 27–28.

8. *Ibid.*, p. 28.

9. Meriol Trevor, *Newman* (New York, 1962), I, 148.

10. *Tracts for the Times* (London, 1833–41), I, 1–2.

11. Of the tracts, Newman was the author of nos. 1, 2, 3, 6, 7, 8, 10, 11, 15, 19, 20, 21, 33, 34, 38, 40, 41, 45, 47, 71, 73, 75, 76, 79, 82, 83, 85, 88, and 90.

12. *Apologia*, pp. 11–15. See also Sylvester P. Juergens, *Newman on the Psychology of Faith in the Individual* (New York, 1928), pp. 72, 167, 176.

13. R. W. Church, *Oxford*, pp. 129–30.

14. Quoted from W. Ward, *Newman*, I, 66.

15. Thomas Mozley, *Reminiscences Chiefly of Oriel College and the Oxford Movement* (London, 1882), I, 313.

16. This work was later published as the first volume of the *Via Media* (London, 1877).

17. *Via Media*, I, 79.

18. *Ibid.*, 137.

19. *Lectures on Justification* (London, 1838).

20. Yngve Brilioth feels that these lectures "form perhaps the chief theological document of the Oxford Movement." See *The Anglican Revival* (London, 1933), p. 282.

21. See *Apologia*, pp. 62–69.

22. *Justification*, p. 340.

23. *Apologia*, p. 68.

24. Eutyches was an abbot of an important monastery during the mid-400s in the outskirts of Constantinople; he is considered the father of Monophysitism.

25. *Apologia*, p. 76.

26. *Ibid.*, p. 78.

27. *Ibid.*, p. 74.

28. *Ibid.*, p. 75.

29. *Tracts*, V, 79.

30. Church, *Oxford*, pp. 298–99.

31. Harrold, *Newman*, p. 43.

32. Brilioth, *Revival*, p. 155.

33. E. A. Knox, *The Tractarian Movement: 1833–1845* (New York, 1933), p. 255.

34. Quoted from Trevor, *Newman*, I, 244.

35. *Ibid.*, pp. 244–45.

36. *Ibid.*, p. 246.

37. *Via Media*, II, 6.

38. Trevor, *Newman*, I, 246.

39. *Apologia*, pp. 89–91.

40. *Ibid.*, p. 93.

41. *Ibid.*, pp. 93–97.

42. *Ibid.*, pp. 114–15.

43. *Ibid.*, pp. 115–17.

44. Quoted from Trevor, *Newman*, I, 303.

45. *Ibid.*, p. 304.

46. For further developments and the revival of the Oxford Movement, see Brilioth, *Revival;* Church, *Oxford;* L. E. Elliott-Binns, *Religion in the Victorian Era* (London, 1936); Knox, *Tractarian;* Shane Leslie, *The Oxford Movement* (Milwaukee, 1933); J. Lewis May, *The Oxford Movement* (London, 1933); J. H. Overton, *The English*

41. *Ibid.*, p. 84.
42. *Ibid.*, p. 120.
43. *Ibid.*, p. 127.
44. *Ibid.*, pp. 188–89.
45. *Ibid.*, pp. 186–87.
46. *Ibid.*, p. 190.
47. *Ibid.*, p. 193.
48. *Ibid.*, p. 195.
49. *Ibid.*, p. 227.
50. *Ibid.*, pp. 227–28.
51. *Ibid.*, p. 221.
52. Fulton Oursler, *The Greatest Faith Ever Known* (New York, 1953), pp. 234, 228.
53. *Idea*, p. 137.
54. *Ibid.*
55. *Ibid.*, p. 232.
56. W. Ward, *Newman*, I, 323–24.
57. For Newman's correspondence on this matter, see *ibid.*, pp. 325–33.
58. Meriol Trevor, *Newman*, II, 47.
59. For a more detailed account of and correspondence involved in the bishopric mystery, see McGrath, *University*, pp. 238–50.
60. *Idea*, p. 277.
61. *Ibid.*, p. 278.
62. The full text of the Rules and Regulations can be found in *My Campaign in Ireland* (London, 1896), pp. 101–45.
63. See McGrath, *University*, pp. 366–67, 462–66, 484–85, 497–499.
64. Ward envisions Newman as rector of a university in "a position involving tasks for which neither his antecedents nor his gifts fitted him." See W. Ward, *Newman*, I, 390. Trevor offers this evaluation: "His work in Dublin has been behind the scenes—it was known to his teaching staff, to a few friends on the spot, but he had made no great public impression." See Trevor, *Newman*, II, 161. McGrath, however, while admitting "certain subtle but definite limitations as an administrator," considers that they were of "minor import." See McGrath, *University*, pp. 507, 509.
65. *Idea*, pp. 472–73.
66. *Ibid.*, p. 453.
67. *Ibid.*, p. 436.
68. *Ibid.*, p. 440.
69. *Ibid.*, pp. 451–52.
70. *Ibid.*, p. 455.
71. *Ibid.*, p. 453.

Church in the Nineteenth Century (London, 1894); W. J. S. Simpson, *The History of the Anglo-Catholic Revival from 1845* (London, 1932); Vernon F. Storr, *The Development of English Theology in the Ninetenth Century: 1800–1860* (London, 1913); C. C. J. Webb, *Religious Thought in the Oxford Movement* (New York, 1928).
47. *Apologia*, p. 145.
48. *Ibid.*, pp. 151–52.
49. Juergens, *Newman*, p. 265.
50. Newman first published the work in 1845, but the *Essay* in this study is examined from the 1878 edition, since this is the form in which Newman desired it to be judged. See Cross, *Newman*, p. 179. For a comparative study of the 1845 and 1878 editions, see Harrold, *Newman*, pp. 394–95.
51. *An Essay on the Development of Christian Doctrine* (London, 1878), pp. 29–30.
52. *Ibid.*, p. 33.
53. *Ibid.*, pp. 41–53.
54. *Ibid.*, p. 37.
55. *Ibid.*, pp. 89–90.
56. *Ibid.*, p. 90.
57. *Ibid.*, p. 97.
58. *Ibid.*, pp. 122–65.
59. *Ibid.*, p. 169.
60. *Ibid.*, p. 170.
61. *Ibid.*, pp. 171–78.
62. *Ibid.*, p. 322.
63. *Ibid.*, pp. 178–85.
64. *Ibid.*, pp. 323–54.
65. *Ibid.*, pp. 185–89.
66. *Ibid.*, pp. 355–83.
67. *Ibid.*, pp. 189–95.
68. *Ibid.*, pp. 383–99.
69. *Ibid.*, pp. 195–99.
70. *Ibid.*, pp. 400–18.
71. *Ibid.*, p. 200.
72. *Ibid.*, pp. 419–36.
73. *Ibid.*, pp. 199–206.
74. *Ibid.*, p. 444.
75. Wilfrid Ward, *Problems and Persons* (London, 1903), p. 9; Guitton, *Philosophie*, pp. 54, 137–40.
76. Barry, *Newman*, p. 278.
77. *Ibid.*, p. 280.
78. R. Blennerhassett, "Some Recollections of Cardinal Newman," *Living Age*, XIII (1901), 796.

79. *Apologia*, p. 152.

80. *Ibid.*, p. 156.

81. W. Ward, *Newman*, I, 161. While he was preparing for the Roman Catholic priesthood in Rome, Newman had the opportunity to discuss his theory on development with a number of outstanding theologians; see *ibid.*, pp. 184–87.

82. *Ibid.*, p. 160.

83. Orestes A. Brownson, "Newman's Development of Christian Doctrine," *Brownson's Works* (Detroit, 1882–87), XIV, 27.

84. *Ibid.*, p. 25.

85. Juergens, *Newman*, p. 265; F. Marin-Sola, *L'évolution homogène du dogme catholique* (Paris, 1924), II, 127; Edmond D. Benard, *A Preface to Newman's Theology* (St. Louis, 1945), pp. 84, 96.

86. Quoted from Lee E. Dirks, *Religion in Action* (Silver Spring, Md.), p. 13.

87. Newman to Robert Wilberforce, October 7, 1845, in W. Ward, *Newman*, I, 92–93.

88. Newman to Spencer Northcote, February, 1846, in *ibid.*, pp. 121–22.

89. *Ibid.*, pp. 125–26.

90. *Ibid.*, pp. 157–69.

91. Newman to J. D. Dalgairns, January 15, 1847, in *ibid.*, p. 176.

92. Ambrose St. John to J. D. Dalgairns and Newman to J. D. Dalgairns, February 24, 1847, in *ibid.*, pp. 181–82.

93. *Loss and Gain: the Story of a Convert* (London, 1848), p. ix.

94. *Ibid.*, p. vii.

95. Joseph E. Baker, *The Novel and the Oxford Movement* (Princeton, N.J., 1932), pp. 62, 64.

96. Harrold, *Newman*, p. 288.

97. Joseph J. Reilly, *Newman as a Man of Letters* (New York, 1925), p. 95.

Chapter Three

1. Newman to Ambrose St. John, July 12, 1848, in W. Ward, *Newman*, I, 202–3.

2. Newman to Bishop Wiseman, October 22, 1848, in *ibid.*, pp. 208–14.

3. See Trevor, *Newman*, I, 452–84, for the details as to the tensions that led to these decisions.

4. *Ibid.*, p. 504.

5. W. Ward, *Newman*, I, 228.

6. Harrold, *Newman*, p. 342.

7. W. Ward, *Newman*, I, 231.

8. *Lectures on Certain Difficulties Felt by Anglicans* 1850, 1872), I, 6.

9. *Ibid.*, p. 47.

10. *Ibid.*, pp. 239–40.

11. *Ibid.*, pp. 261–95.

12. *Ibid.*, pp. 296–362.

13. John E. Ross, *John Henry Newman* (New York, 19

14. Hutton, *Newman*, p. 207.

15. Wilfrid Ward, *Life and Times of Cardinal Wisema* 1897), I, 542.

16. For Newman's reaction to Wiseman's pastoral W. Ward, I, 256–57.

17. *Lectures on the Present Position of Catholics in Eng* don, 1851), p. ix.

18. W. Ward, *Newman*, I, 264.

19. *Position*, p. 41.

20. *Ibid.*, p. 45.

21. *Ibid.*, p.131.

22. See W. Ward, *Newman*, I, 264.

23. Ross, *Newman*, p. 65.

24. *Position*, pp. 208–9.

25. London *Times*, June 25, 1852.

26. Newman to Sister Imelda Poole, July 4, 1852, in *Newman*, I, 294.

27. *The Second Spring* (London, 1911), p. 27.

28. *Ibid.*, pp. 35, 36.

29. *Letters of Archbishop Ullathorne*, p. 29, quoted p. 41.

30. W. Ward, *Newman*, II, 60.

31. Quoted from Francis P. Donnelly, in Newman, *Sp*

32. For a detailed historical account, see Fergal Mc *man's University: Idea and Reality* (London, 1951), pp

33. Heron estimates that fifteen out of a Catholic seven million attended a university between 1794 an Denis C. Heron, *Constitutional History of the Universi* (Dublin, 1847), pp. 93–94.

34. McGrath, *University*, p. 77.

35. Quoted from *ibid.*, p. 101.

36. *The Idea of a University* (New York, 1941), p.

37. *Ibid.*

38. *Ibid.*, p. 44.

39. *Ibid.*, p. 62.

40. *Ibid.*, pp. 67–68.

72. *Ibid.*, p. 444.
73. *Ibid.*, p. 445.
74. *Ibid.*, p. 450.
75. "A Form of Infidelity of the Day," in *Idea*, pp. 395–99.
76. *Ibid.*, pp. 309–409.
77. "Elementary Studies," in *Idea*, pp. 347–48.
78. *Ibid.*, p. 354.
79. "Literature," in *Idea*, p. 292.
80. *Ibid.*, p. 293.
81. *Ibid.*
82. *Ibid.*, p. 301.
83. "English Catholic Literature," in *Idea*, p. 322.
84. *Ibid.*, p. 323.
85. See Trevor, *Newman*, II, 55–156.
86. McGrath, *University*, p. 439.
87. W. Ward, *Newman*, I, 370–74.
88. McGrath, *University*, p. 441.
89. *Ibid.*, pp. 441–43, 446–48.
90. *Ibid.*, pp. 490–6.
91. Bertrand Newman, *Cardinal Newman: a Biographical and Literary Study* (New York, 1925), p. 128.
92. Barry, *Newman*, p. 108.
93. McGrath, *University*, p. 444.
94. *Ibid.*, p. 510.
95. *Ibid.*, pp. 509–10.
96. See *ibid.*, p. 504, and W. Ward, *Newman*, II, 192.
97. *Callista: a Sketch of the Third Century* (New York, 1855), p. iv.
98. *Ibid.*, p. iii.
99. *Ibid.*
100. Harrold, *Newman*, pp. 286, 288.
101. Reilly, *Newman*, p. 95.
102. *Callista*, pp. 133, 134, 136, 137.

Chapter Four

1. Newman to Wiseman, September 14, 1857, in W. Ward, *Newman*, I, 419.
2. *Ibid.*, pp. 425–26.
3. *Ibid.*, p. 427.
4. *Ibid.*, pp. 428–29.
5. *Ibid.*, pp. 350, 418.
6. Newman to W. K. Sullivan, November 30, 1858, in *ibid.*, p. 432.
7. This article was republished in *Historical Sketches*, II, under the title, "The Benedictine Schools."

8. *Historical Sketches* (London, 1872), II, 452–53.

9. *Ibid.*, pp. 475–76.

10. *Ibid.*, p. 475.

11. *Ibid.*, p. 476.

12. Sir John Acton to Newman, July 8, 1861, in W. Ward, *Newman*, I, 532.

13. See *ibid.*, pp. 243–51.

14. Newman to Ambrose St. John, May 7, 1857, in *ibid.*, p. 437.

15. *Ibid.*, p. 438.

16. Newman to Capes, May 17, 1858, in *ibid.*, p. 439. Newman to Capes, August 18, 1858, in *ibid.*, pp. 440–43.

17. See *ibid.*, p. 493.

18. Trevor, *Newman*, II, 196.

19. "Judgment of the English Bishops," *The Rambler*, May, 1859, p. 122.

20. John Coulson, in introduction to J. H. Newman, *On Consulting the Faithful in Matters of Doctrine* (New York, 1961), pp. 9–12.

21. S. Nasmyth Stokes, "Royal Commission on Education," *The Rambler*, January, 1859, p. 17.

22. "Judgment," pp. 122–23.

23. Newman, Memorandum of May 22, 1859, quoted from Samuel D. Femiano, *Infallibility of the Laity* (New York, 1967), p. 97.

24. *Consulting*, pp. 53–54.

25. *Ibid.*, pp. 54–55.

26. *Ibid.*, p. 63.

27. *Ibid.*

28. *Ibid.*, pp. 63–74.

29. *Ibid.*, pp. 74–76.

30. *Ibid.*, pp. 77–101.

31. Trevor, *Newman*, II, 208.

32. *Ibid.*, pp. 204–5.

33. Newman to Henry Wilberforce, July, 1859, in W. Ward, *Newman*, I, 573.

34. Newman to Sir John Acton, June 20, 1861, in *ibid.*, p. 523.

35. See Trevor, *Newman*, II, 216–21.

36. Newman to Miss E. Bowles, May 19, 1863, in W. Ward, I, 586. Reflecting on his going to Rome, Newman wrote: "This age of the Church is peculiar. In former times there was not the extreme centralization now in use. If a private theologian said anything free, another answered him. If the controversy grew, then it went to a bishop. The Holy See was but the court of ultimate appeal. *Now* if I as a private priest put anything into print, Propaganda answers me at once. How can I fight with such a chain on my arm? It is like the Persians driven to fight under the lash. There was true private judgment

in the primitive and medieval schools—there are no schools now, no private judgment (in the religious sense of the phrase), no freedom, that is, of opinion. That is, no exercise of the intellect. No, the system goes on by the tradition of the intellect of former times." Quoted from John A. O'Brien, *Giants of the Faith* (New York, 1960), pp. 173–74.

37. W. Ward, *Newman*, I, 573.

38. Newman to Henry Wilberforce, July, 1859, in *ibid.*, p. 573.

39. For details in this endeavor of Newman, see Trevor, *Newman*, II, 248–64.

40. Newman to William Neville, March 27, 1862, in W. Ward, *Newman*, I, 579.

41. See *ibid.*, pp. 580–89.

42. Quoted from Trevor, *Newman*, II, 265.

43. *Ibid.*, p. 266.

44. W. Ward, *Newman*, I, 568.

45. *Verses*, p. 319.

Chapter Five

1. *Apologia*, p. vi.

2. *Ibid.*

3. *Ibid.* The sermon in question, "Wisdom and Innocence," is contained in Newman's *Sermons on Subjects of the Day* (London, 1843).

4. *Ibid.*, pp. vi-vii.

5. Quoted from W. Ward, *Newman*, II, 8.

6. *Apologia*, pp. 140–41, 215–16.

7. W. Ward, *Newman*, II, 18–19.

8. Newman to Frederick Rogers, April 22, 1864, in *ibid.*, p. 19; Newman to R. W. Church, April 23, 1864, in *ibid.*, pp. 19–20; Newman to R. W. Church, April 26, 1864, in *ibid.*, p. 21; Newman to John Keble, April 27, 1864, in *ibid.*, p. 22; Newman to Rogers, May 1, 1864, in *ibid.*, pp. 23–24; Newman to Church, May 2, 1864, in *ibid.*, p. 24.

9. *Ibid.*, p. 23.

10. *Apologia*, pp. 1–2.

11. Since the *Apologia* has been considered along with the other writings and thought of the author in the presentation of his theological development, an analysis of it is not required. Any study of Newman, however, would be inadequate without reading it, as the hopes and aspirations, the main events of his life up to his conversion to Roman Catholicism, the authors and persons who have influenced him—all are contained in this autobiography.

12. Harrold, *Newman*, p. 307.

13. Quoted from W. Ward, *Newman*, II, 33.

14. Knox, *Tractarian*, p. vii.

15. William T. Noon, "Newman's 'Apologia'—1965," *America*, CXII (1965), 631.

16. Harrold, *Newman*, p. 317.

17. See Cuthbert Butler, *The Life and Times of Bishop Ullathorne* (London, 1926), I, 332.

18. A. F. Hort, *Life and Letters of Fenton John Anthony Hort* (London, 1896), II, 423–25.

19. A. M. Fairbairn, *Catholicism: Roman and Anglican* (London, 1889), p. 241.

20. Knox, *Tractarian*, p. vii.

21. Newman to Sir William Cope, February 13, 1875, in W. Ward, *Newman*, II, 46.

22. Talbot to Newman, July 24, 1864; Newman to Talbot, July 25, 1864, in *ibid.*, p. 539.

23. *Ibid.*, p. 47.

24. See Newman's "Memorandum," in *ibid.*, p. 76; Newman to Father Coleridge, December 30, 1864, in *ibid.*, p. 77.

25. Newman to T. W. Allies, January 17, 1865, in *ibid.*, p. 78.

26. *Ibid.*

27. *The Dream of Gerontius* (London, 1916), pp. 17, 18.

28. *Ibid.*, p. 27.

29. *Ibid.*, p. 36.

30. *Ibid.*, p. 51.

31. *Ibid.*, p. 56.

32. *Ibid.*, pp. 57, 58.

33. *Ibid.*, p. 59.

34. *Ibid.*, p. 61.

35. Reilly is of the opinion that "Had he [Newman] been asked how much time he had spent on *Gerontius*, he might truthfully have answered, not 'A few weeks,' but rather, 'All my life.'" See *Newman*, p. 132.

36. Harrold, *Newman*, p. 278.

37. *Verses*, pp. v–vi.

38. "Introductory Notes," *Gerontius*, p. 10.

39. Harrold, *Newman*, p. 283.

40. *Apologia*, pp. 157–58.

41. Newman to Hope-Scott, August 29, 1864, in W. Ward, *Newman*, II, 51–52, 54–55.

42. *Ibid.*, pp. 64–65.

43. *Ibid.*, pp. 65–68.

44. *Ibid.*, p. 122.

45. *Ibid.*, p. 131.

46. *Ibid.*, pp. 131–32.

47. *Ibid.*, pp. 138–39.

48. Newman to Coleridge, April 26, 1867, in *ibid.*, II, 141–42.

49. Ambrose St. John to Newman, May 1, 1867, in *ibid.*, II, 160–163.

50. Newman to Bishop Ullathorne, August 18, 1867, and Ullathorne to Newman, August 19, 1867, in *ibid.*, II, 184–85.

51. Newman to Pusey, October 31, 1865, in *ibid.*, II, 100.

52. *Ibid.*

53. Newman informed Pusey of the public reply the day after he had written it. See *ibid.*, p. 102.

54. *Ibid.*, pp. 102–3.

55. *Ibid.*, p. 100.

56. *Letter to the Rev. E. B. Pusey on his Recent "Eirenicon"* (London, 1866), pp. 6–7.

57. *Ibid.*, pp. 9–25.

58. Harrold, *Newman*, p. 205.

59. *Eirenicon*, p. 31.

60. *Ibid.*, p. 32.

61. *Ibid.*, pp. 33–34.

62. *Ibid.*, p. 36.

63. *Ibid.*, pp. 47–48.

64. *Ibid.*, pp. 62–63.

65. *Ibid.*, pp. 63–67.

66. *Ibid.*, pp. 113–14.

67. *Ibid.*, p. 79.

68. *Ibid.*, p. 17, footnote. Newman's opposition to the stand of Manning and Ward will be treated in the section on papal infallibility.

69. London *Times*, March 31, 1866.

70. Newman to Pusey, April 2, 1866, in W. Ward, *Newman*, II, 113.

71. See Trevor, *Newman*, II, 379, and Shane Leslie, *Henry Edward Manning: His Life and Labours* (New York, 1921), pp. 274–77.

72. Trevor, *Newman*, II, 380.

73. Newman to Pusey, April 2, 1866, in W. Ward, *Newman*, II, 113.

74. *Ibid.*, p. 114.

75. *Ibid.*, p. 115.

76. Newman to Dr. Meynell, January 23, 1860, in *ibid.*, II, 243.

77. *Apologia*, p. 7.

78. *Ibid.*, pp. 13–14.

79. *Fifteen Sermons Preached before the University of Oxford* (London, 1909), pp. 16–36, 57–74, 176–201, 202–221, 251–277, 278–311.

80. *Lectures on Justification*, p. 267.
81. W. Ward, *Newman*, I, 394.
82. Newman to Aubrey de Vere, August, 1870, in *ibid.*, II, 245.
83. Newman to Dr. Meynell, February 20, 1870, in *ibid.*, II, 261.
84. Benard, *Preface*, p. 159.
85. Juergens, *Newman*, pp. 17–18; Harrold, *Newman*, p. 131.
86. *An Essay in Aid of a Grammar of Assent* (London, 1870), p. 14.
87. *Ibid.*
88. *Ibid.*, pp. 36–41.
89. *Ibid.*, pp. 37, 40.
90. *Ibid.*, pp. 89–91.
91. *Ibid.*, pp. 157–58, 191–95.
92. *Ibid.*, p. 221.
93. *Ibid.*, p. 220.
94. *Ibid.*, p. 239.
95. *Ibid.*, p. 288.
96. *Ibid.*, p. 411.
97. Thomas Harper, "Dr. Newman's Essay in Aid of a Grammar of Assent," *The Month*, XII (1870), 599–611, 667–92.
98. *Grammar*, p. 112.
99. *Ibid.*, p. 72.
100. Newman to Brownlow, April 13, 1870, in W. Ward, *Newman*, II, 269.
101. *Grammar*, p. 104.
102. *Ibid.*, pp. 117–18.
103. W. Ward, *Newman*, II, 271–74.
104. Christopher Hollis, *Newman and the Modern World* (New York, 1968), p. 180.
105. John F. Cronin, *Cardinal Newman: His Theory of Knowledge* (Washington, 1935), p. xiv.
106. W. Ward, *Newman*, II, 400.
107. A similar movement existed in France under the leadership of Louis Veuillot, editor of the periodical, *L'Univers*.
108. Ward's son quoted his father as saying, "I should like a new Papal Bull every morning with my *Times* at breakfast." See W. Ward, *Newman*, II, 213.
109. Benard, *Preface*, p. 58.
110. *Difficulties*, II, 176, 177.
111. *Ibid.*, pp. 324–25.
112. *Ibid.*, p. 256.
113. *Ibid.*, p. 257.
114. *Ibid.*, p. 255.
115. *Ibid.*, pp. 248, 250, 257.
116. *Ibid.*, pp. 250, 257–58.

117. *Ibid.*, pp. 256–57.

118. *Ibid.*, pp. 240–42.

119. See W. Ward, *Newman*, II, 406–7, and Newman to Lord Blachford, April 11, 1875, in *ibid.*, pp. 407–9.

120. Walter M. Abbott, ed., *The Documents of Vatican II* (New York, 1966), pp. 48–9, 213–14, 675–96. For an impact of Newman's views today, see also A. B. Calkins, "John Henry Newman on Conscience and the Magisterium," *The Downside Review* (October, 1969), pp. 358–69.

121. *Via Media* (London, 1877), I, xlii.

122. *Ibid.*, p. xliii; see also W. Ward, *Newman*, II, 423.

123. *Ibid.*, p. xx.

124. *Ibid.*, p. xxxii.

125. *Ibid.*, p. liii.

126. Newman to Lord Blachford, May 31, 1875, in W. Ward, *Newman*, II, 410–14.

127. *Ibid.*, p. 426.

128. Duke of Norfolk to W. Ward, in *ibid.*, pp. 436–38.

129. Newman to Bishop Ullathorne, February 2, 1879, in *ibid.*, pp. 439–40.

130. Newman to Dean Church, March 11, 1879, in *ibid.*, p. 451.

131. Ullathorne to Cardinal Manning, March 4, 1879, in *ibid.*, pp. 446–47.

132. Manning to Newman, March 8, 1879, in *ibid.*, p. 449.

133. Quoted from *ibid.*, p.464.

134. *Ibid.*, p. 503.

135. Principal Fairbairn, "Catholicism and Religious Thought," *Contemporary Review* (May, 1885), p. 667.

136. "The Development of Religious Error," *Contemporary Review* (October, 1885), p. 850.

Chapter Six

1. "Literature," in *Idea*, p. 296.

2. *Ibid.*, p. 306.

3. *Ibid.*, p. 307.

4. Reilly, *Newman*, p. 302.

5. Quoted from *ibid.*

6. "Literature," in *Idea*, pp. 307–8.

7. Reilly, *Newman*, p. 303.

8. Amy Cruse, *The Victorians and Their Reading* (New York, 1935), p. 116.

9. Fernande Tardivel, *La personnalité littéraire de Newman* (Paris, 1937), p. 316: "Comme elles nous semblent étrangères aux élans de Bossuet, aux exultations de Lacordaire! Il n'est qu'à rapprocher le

Panégyrique de sainte Thérèse ou le célèbre sermon sur l'amour de quelques-uns des passages les plus chaleureux de Newman pour apprécier pleinement la réserve propre à ses moments d'effusion." See also Barry, *Newman*, pp. 52, 155–56.

10. Quoted from Mozley, *Letters*, II, 219.

11. "University Preaching," in *Idea*, 416.

12. *Ibid.*, pp. 416–17.

13. *Ibid.*, pp. 417–18.

14. Harrold, *Newman*, p. 319.

15. Mozley, *Letters*, II, 477.

16. "Literature," in *Idea*, pp. 297–98.

17. Giovanni Costigan, *Makers of Modern England* (New York, 1967), p. ix. Costigan also regards Newman as one of the seven makers of modern England and as "the chief religious figure of nineteenth-century England." See pp. ix-xii, 51.

18. Arthur Bestor, *The Restoration of Learning* (New York, 1955), p. 58.

19. Christopher Dawson, *Understanding Europe* (New York, 1955), pp. 242, 243.

20. Edward E. Kelly, "Newman, Vatican I and II, and the Church Today," *The Catholic World*, CCII (1966), 291.

21. *Ibid.*

22. Newman, *Difficulties*, I. 261. See also Pope John XXIII's Encyclical Letter, "Ad Petri Cathedram," in *The 1960 National Catholic Almanac* (Paterson, N.J., 1960), p. 170.

23. Pope Paul VI, "These Two Holy Figures," *Herder Correspondence*, I (1964), 29, 30.

24. Kelly, "Newman," p. 293; Hans Kung, *The Council, Reform and Reunion* (New York, 1961), pp. 26–7, 72, 85, 89, 94, 119, 126, 162.

25. Kelly, "Newman," p. 293; Hans Kung, Yves Congar, Daniel O'Hanlon, ed., *Council Speeches of Vatican II* (Glen Rock, N.J., 1964), pp. 181, 206, 285.

26. See previous chapter, section on papal infallibility.

27. "Dogmatic Constitution of the Church," in Walter M. Abbott, ed., *The Documents of Vatican II* (New York, 1966), pp. 42–47.

28. "Decree on the Apostolate of the Laity," in *ibid.*, pp. 491–521.

29. "Declaration on Religious Freedom," in *ibid.*, pp. 675–96.

30. Quoted from Kelly, "Newman," p. 293.

31. Quoted from *ibid.*, p. 292.

32. Christopher Hollis has expressed a similar view: "He is not . . . a party leader today. His influence is not confined to the progressive majority in the Council. The conservative minority and those who with the Pope have been working to prevent divisions in the Church have

equally been able to find their inspiration from his work. It would be a great mistake if, to apply the present phraseology, we sought to label . . . Newman as a progressive. In this, as in all things, Newman's way was always the middle way. In the present controversies the progressives no doubt have the better of the argument but it is necessary to appreciate the fear of honest conservatives who think that there is a danger that in the passions of *aggiornamento* the progressives will abandon the whole claim of the Church to be the uniquely divine institution and see it as merely one among a number of religious bodies. If there be such a fear and if there be on occasion reason for such fear, it goes without saying that there is no difficulty in finding passage after passage in Newman which insists on the necessity of the Church to assert without qualification her divine nature. Between the two extremes stands Newman, asserting alike the just rights of authority and the supremacy of reason, in his wider sense of the word." See *Newman,* p. 214.

33. *London Quarterly Review,* March, 1846.

34. J. A. Froude, *Short Studies on Great Subjects* (New York, 1883), IV, 282–83.

35. Harrold, *Newman,* p. 352.

36. Herbert L. Stewart, *A Century of Anglo-Catholicism* (London, 1929), p. 122.

37. E. B. Burgum, "Cardinal Newman and the Complexity of Truth," *Sewanee Review,* XXXVIII (1930), 320.

38. *Historical Sketches* (London, 1872), III, 59.

39. *Apologia,* p. 3.

40. C. J. Callan, "Cardinal Newman as a Promising Candidate for the Twofold Title of Saint and Doctor of the Church," *America,* November 22, 1941.

Selected Bibliography

PRIMARY SOURCES

I. Bibliographies

BATESON, E. W., ed. *Cambridge Bibliography of English Literature* (Cambridge, England, 1941), III, 686–91.

GILLOW, JOSEPH. *Bibliographical Dictionary of the English Catholics* (London, 1941), V, 165–74.

The Guide to Catholic Literature (Detroit, 1940–67), I, 840–44; II, 415–16; III, 430–32; IV, 681–82; V, 514–15; VI, 483–85; VII, 788–89; VIII, 279.

HARROLD, CHARLES F. *John Henry Newman* (New York, 1945), pp. 440–52. Valuable for its extensive background and related sources for Newman and his historical milieu.

II. Manuscript Materials

Birmingham Oratory Archives, England. Contains letters by and to Newman, his autobiographical memoranda and private diaries, unpublished sermons and sermon notes, newspaper clippings, and manuscripts of periodical articles and lectures.

London Oratory Archives, England. Contains correspondence and memoranda of Faber and Dalgairns, some of which refer to Newman, and documents relating to the quarrel between the Birmingham and London Oratories (1855–56), with memoranda by Newman. A more detailed description of the contents of both archives can be found in Meriol Trevor, *Newman* (New York, 1962), I, 639–41.

III. Works by Newman

Apologia pro Vita Sua. London: Longmans, Green & Co., 1864.

The Arians of the Fourth Century. London: Rivingtons, 1833.

Callista: a Sketch of the Third Century. London: Burns & Oates, 1855.

The Church of the Fathers. London: Rivingtons, 1842.

Discourses on the Scope and Nature of a University Education. Dublin: Burns & Lamb, 1852.

Discourses to Mixed Congregations. London: Longmans, Green & Co., 1849.

Discussions and Arguments. London: Longmans, Green & Co., 1872.

The Dream of Gerontius. London: Longmans, Green & Co., 1865.

Essay on the Miracles Recorded in the Ecclesiastical History of the Early Ages. London: Rivingtons, 1843.

An Essay in Aid of a Grammar of Assent. London: Longmans, Green & Co., 1870.

An Essay on the Development of Christian Doctrine. London: James Toovey, 1845, 1878.

Essays Critical and Historical. 2 vols. London: Longmans, Green & Co., 1872.

Historical Sketches. 3 vols. London: Longmans, Green & Co., 1872.

The Idea of a University. London: Longmans, Green & Co., 1852.

Lectures on Certain Difficulties Felt by Anglicans. London: Burns & Lambert, 1850.

Lectures on Justification. London: Rivingtons, 1838.

Lectures on the Present Position of Catholics in England. London: Burns & Lambert, 1851.

Lectures on the Prophetical Office of the Church, Viewed Relatively to Romanism and Popular Protestantism. London: Rivingtons, 1838.

Letter to the Duke of Norfolk. London: Pickering, 1875.

Letter to the Rev. E. B. Pusey on his Recent "Eirenicon." London: Longmans, Green & Co., 1866.

Loss and Gain: the Story of a Convert. London: Jas. Burns, 1848.

Meditations and Devotions. London: Longmans, Green & Co., 1893.

My Campaign in Ireland. London: Aberdeen, A. King & Co., 1896.

The Office and Work of the Universities. London: Longman, Brown, Green, and Longmans, 1856.

Oxford University Sermons. London: Rivingtons, 1843.

Parochial and Plain Sermons. 8 vols. London: Rivingtons, 1834–43.

Sermons on Subjects of the Day. London: Rivingtons, 1843.

Sermons Preached on Various Occasions. London: Burns & Lamb, 1852.

Tracts Theological and Ecclesiastical. London: Longmans, Green & Co., 1874.

Verses on Various Occasions. London: Longmans, Green & Co., 1868.

Via Media. 2 vols. London: Longmans, Green & Co., 1877, 1883.

Works of John Henry Newman. 40 vols. London: Longmans, Green & Co., 1874–1921.

IV. Compilations of Newman's Works

Addresses to Cardinal Newman, with His Replies. Edited by William P. Neville. London: Longmans, Green & Co., 1905.

Cardinal Newman and William Froude: a Correspondence. Edited by Gordon H. Harper. Baltimore: Johns Hopkins Press, 1933.

Correspondence of John Henry Newman with John Keble and Others, 1839–1845. Edited by the Fathers of the Birmingham Oratory. London: Longmans, Green & Co., 1917. A compilation of correspondence in the last six years of Newman as an Anglican.

The Essential Newman. Edited by Vincent Blehe. New York: The New American Library, 1963.

Faith and Prejudice, and Other Unpublished Sermons. Edited by the Fathers of the Birmingham Oratory. New York: Sheed & Ward, 1956.

Favorite Newman Sermons. Edited by Daniel M. O'Connell. Milwaukee: Bruce, 1932.

The Fine Gold of Newman. Edited by Joseph J. Reilly. New York: Macmillan Co., 1931.

The Idea of a Liberal Education: a Selection from the Works of Newman. Edited by Henry Tristam. London: Harrap, 1952.

Index to the Works of John Henry Cardinal Newman. Edited by Joseph J. Rickaby. London: Longmans, Green & Co., 1914. An indispensable source for integrating Newman's views expressed at different times in his life.

John Henry Newman: Autobiographical Writings. Edited by Henry Tristam. New York: Sheed & Ward, 1957.

John Henry Newman: with a Set of Unpublished Letters. Edited by Frank Leslie Cross. London: Longmans, Green & Co., 1933. Valuable for a view of Oxford in Newman's time.

Letters and Correspondence of John Henry Newman During His Life in the English Church, with a Brief Autobiography. Edited by Anne Mozley. London: Longmans, Green & Co., 1891. 2 vols. Compiled and edited, at Newman's request, by his sister; especially useful for his early life.

Letters and Diaries of John Henry Newman. Edited by Charles S. Dessain. London: T. Nelson, 1961–68. 17 vols.

Mr. Kingsley and Dr. Newman: a Correspondence on the Question whether Dr. Newman teaches that Truth is no Virtue? London: Longmans, Green & Co., 1864.

Newman at St. Mary's: a Selection of the Plain and Parochial Sermons. Edited by Lawrence F. Barmann. Westminster, Md.: Newman Press, 1962.

A Newman Reader. Edited by Francis X. Connolly. New York: Double-
day & Co., 1964.
A Newman Synthesis. Edited by Erich Przywara. New York: Long-
mans, Green & Co., 1931.
A Newman Treasury. Edited by Charles F. Harrold. London: Long-
mans, Green & Co., 1943.
Philosophical Readings in Cardinal Newman. Edited by James Collins.
Chicago: H. Regnery Co., 1961.
Sermon Notes of John Henry Cardinal Newman, 1849–1878. Edited
by the Fathers of the Birmingham Oratory. London: Longmans,
Green & Co., 1913.

SECONDARY SOURCES

BARRY, WILLIAM F. *Newman.* New York: C. Scribner's and Sons,
1905. Short biography; useful as an introduction to the study of
Newman.
BENARD, EDMOND D. *A Preface to Newman's Theology.* St. Louis:
Herder & Co., 1945. Analytical approach to set forth Newman's
theological thinking in systematic fashion.
BOEKRAAD, A. J. *The Personal Conquest of Truth According to Newman.* Louvain, Belgium: Éditions Nauwelaerts, 1955. Interesting
study of Newman's intellectual ideals and his unlimited dedica-
tion to truth.
BOUYER, LOUIS. *Newman, His Life and Spirituality.* New York: P. J.
Kennedy, 1958. Newman's life examined in the light of his Christian ideals and virtues.
BROWNSON, ORESTES A. "Newman's Development of Christian Doctrine," *Brownson's Works.* Detroit: Thorndike Nourse, 1882–87.
Newman's Catholicism questioned by a convert to Roman Catholicism in respect to the development theory. XIV, 1–28.
BURGUM, E. B. "Cardinal Newman and the Complexity of Truth,"
Sewanee Review, XXXVIII (1930), 128–33. Unsuccessful, biased
attempt to present Newman as limited in his outlook towards
social problems.
CALKINS, ARTHUR BURTON. "John Henry Newman on Conscience and
the Magisterium," *The Downside Review,* LXXXVII (1969),
358–69. Excellent essay on a topic of great interest today by a
young Newman scholar.
CHAPMAN, H. J. "Newman and the Fathers," *Blackfriars,* XIV (1933),
578–90. Scholarly presentation of Newman's indebtedness to the
Fathers of the Church.
CHURCH, R. W. *The Oxford Movement.* Hamden, Conn.: Archon
Books, 1966. A reprint, originally published in 1892; regarded as

a classic in the study of the religious thought at Oxford University in the first half of the nineteenth century.

CORCORAN, TIMOTHY. "Liberal Studies and Moral Aims: a Critical Study of Newman's Position," *Thought*, I (1926), 54–71. Presents Newman as an overestimated humanist philosopher of education, without adequately providing for theology's preeminence; position untenable.

COULSON, JOHN. *Theology and the University*. London: Darton, Longman, and Todd, 1964. Analysis of Newman's plan for an educated laity.

CRONIN, JOHN F. *Cardinal Newman: His Theory of Knowledge*. Washington: Catholic University of America Press, 1935. Scholarly examination of the sources that influenced Newman's formulation of his theory of knowledge.

CULLER, A. DWIGHT. *The Imperial Intellect*. New Haven, Conn.: Yale University Press, 1955. Study of Newman's educational ideals.

EVANS, JOHN WHITNEY. "Newman, Education, and the Place of the Laity," *The Catholic Educator*, XXXVI (1965), 33–35. Timely in the light of Vatican Council II.

FENTON, JOHN C. "Some Newman Autobiographical Sketches and the Newman Legend," *American Ecclesiastical Review*, CXXXVI (1957), 394–410. Among the relatively few who feel that Newman has been "idolized" rather than studied; position untenable.

GUITTON, JEAN. *The Church and the Laity: from Newman to Vatican II*. Staten Island, N.Y.: Alba House, 1965. Extensive treatment of the impact of Newman's thought and influence on the role of the laity in the Roman Catholic Church.

————. *La philosophie de Newman: essai sur l'idée de développement*. Paris: Aubier Éditions Montaigne, 1933. Study of Newman's theory of development in the total context of his thought.

HARPER, THOMAS. "Dr. Newman's Essay in Aid of a Grammar of Assent," *The Month*, XII (1870), 599–611, 667–92. Contemporary's critique of Newman's rational basis for religious faith.

HARROLD, CHARLES F. *John Henry Newman*. New York: Longmans, Green & Co., 1945. Best study of Newman by an Anglican; objective and accurate.

————. "Newman and the Alexandrian Platonists," *Modern Philology*, XXXVII (1940), 279–91. Attempt to show the influence of the Greek Fathers of the Church and Platonism upon Newman.

HOLLIS, CHRISTOPHER. *Newman and the Modern World*. New York: Doubleday & Co., 1968. Appraisal of the life and thought of Newman, with their impact on twentieth-century Christianity.

HUTTON, RICHARD H. *Cardinal Newman*. Boston: Houghton, Mifflin

& Co., 1891. Biography written by a contemporary; highly favorable appraisal of Newman's life and personality.

JENNINGS, HENRY J. *Cardinal Newman.* Birmingham, England: Houghton & Co., 1882. Contains numerous details about Newman not found elsewhere; written by a contemporary and a friend.

JUERGENS, SYLVESTER F. *Newman on the Psychology of Faith in the Individual.* New York: Macmillan Co., 1928. Thorough analysis of the *Grammar of Assent,* with the influences and sources that led to its formulation.

KELLY, EDWARD E. "Newman, Vatican I and II, and the Church Today," *The Catholic World,* CCII (1966), 291–97. Presents relevance of Newman's thinking to the present day.

McGRATH, FERGAL. *Newman's University: Idea and Reality.* London: Longmans, Green & Co., 1951. Well-documented analysis of the background, planning, history, and evaluation of the Catholic University of Dublin.

MOZLEY, HARRIET. *Family Adventures.* London: John and Charles Murphy, 1852. Interesting descriptions of the Newman family by Newman's sister; particularly helpful for Newman's youthful days.

MOZLEY, THOMAS. *Reminiscences Chiefly of Oriel College and the Oxford Movement.* London: Longmans, Green & Co., 1882. 2 vols. A brother's-in-law account of Newman during his early Oxford days.

NOON, WILLIAM T. "Newman's 'Apologia'—1965," *America,* CXII (1965), 631–36. Presentation of the special relevance of Newman's spiritual autobiography in a time of ecumenism.

O'FAOLAIN, SEAN. *Newman's Way.* London: Longmans, Green & Co., 1952. Description of Newman's mind in successive steps that led to his conversion to Roman Catholicism.

PATTISON, MARK. *Memoirs.* London: H. Nettleship, 1885. Objective, unbiased memoranda by an early follower of Newman.

PAUL VI, POPE. "These Two Holy Figures," *Herder Correspondence,* I (1964), 28–30. Timely encomium of Newman by the Catholic Church's reigning pontiff.

REILLY, JOSEPH J. *Newman as a Man of Letters.* New York: Macmillan Co., 1925. Appraisal of the different media of literary expression employed by Newman.

ROSS, JOHN E. *John Henry Newman.* New York: E. W. Norton & Co., 1933. Biographical study of Newman as an Anglican minister.

RYAN, ALVAN S. "The Development of Newman's Political Thought," *Review of Politics,* VII (1945), 210–40. Formulation of Newman's political thought as it is affected in the crucible of historical experience.

————. *Newman and Gladstone: the Vatican Decrees.* Notre Dame, Ind.: University of Notre Dame Press, 1962.

TREVOR, MERIOL. *Newman.* New York: Doubleday & Co., 1962, 2 vols. Considered a definitive study of Newman's life; although scholarly, lacks precise documentation.

WARD, MAISIE. *Young Mr. Newman.* New York: Sheed & Ward, 1948. Thorough study of Newman's life to the age of forty-four; particularly helpful for insights into the influence of family and experiences at Oxford upon later life.

WARD, WILFRID. *The Life of John Henry Cardinal Newman.* London: Longmans, Green & Co., 1913. 2 vols. Full-length biography based on Newman's private correspondence and journals; long considered the standard biography of Newman.

Index